Going Deeper in Jesus

2017

By Dr. Delron Shirley
Cover Design by Jeremy Shirley

This teaching manual is intended for personal study; however, the author encourages all students to also become teachers and to share the truths from this text with others. However, copying the text itself without permission from the author is considered plagiarism, which is punishable by law. To obtain permission to quote material from this book, please contact:

Delron Shirley
3210 Cathedral Spires Dr.
Colorado Springs, CO 80904
www.teachallnationsmission.com
teachallnations@msn.com

Day 1

Going Deeper in Jesus

The other day, someone mentioned to me her desire to "go deeper in Jesus." The image that immediately flashed into my mind was an illustrated sermon that one of my students had presented in a children's meeting on a recent mission trip. She had a beautifully wrapped gift box with several other equally attractive gift boxes inside. Based on the reference in II Corinthians 9:15 that salvation is a gift, she opened the big box to see what was inside when she accepted the gift of salvation. Of course, the other boxes inside represented a the many other spiritual benefits that the Bible also describes as gifts – righteousness (Romans 5:17), eternal life (Romans 6:23), grace (Ephesians 3:9), and the gifts off the Spirit (I Corinthians 12:4). With this imagery in mind, I envisioned an antique chest that my grandmother had when I was a little child. Always imagining that it was a pirate's treasure chest, my cousins and I always wanted to have the chance to look inside. Suddenly I could envision that the lady who wanted to "go deeper in Jesus" had finally found the key to that mysterious old chest, and I could picture her bending over the open box pulling out one item after another – trying to get to the bottom to find the last treasure that was hidden in it.

With this vision in mind, I turned to my Bible to see what it describes as the things are to be discovered when we begin to explore what is in Jesus. To do so, I looked up all the verses that reference "in Christ" and "in Him." To my surprise, there were over a hundred such references – and I'd like to take the time to explore a few of the most significant ones. In doing so, hopefully we can all go a little deeper in Jesus. Join me on this journey.

Day 2

All Fullness is in Christ

The first verse that I'd like to look at is Colossians 1:19 that tells us that it pleased God that all fullness should dwell in Jesus. I couldn't help myself from interpreting that verse with the image of a scene from a circus clown act when one of the clowns opens a box and a bunch of coiled snakes pop out like a Jack-in-the-box. Of course the other clowns all stand around and laugh at the shock of the one who unwittingly opened the lid. They had taken pleasure in pulling the prank on their friend. Of course, God was not joking when He took pleasure in packing Jesus so full of blessings that they just spring out at us when we begin to explore what it means to live in Him. Of course, all of us have experienced this sort of thing when we open a piece of merchandise that was packaged at the factory. Once we take it out of the box, there is no possible way to get all the merchandise and the packing material back into the original box. I've always assumed that this was the manufacture's way of ensuring that we would not be able to return the product for a refund since one of the requirements to get our money back is that it has to be returned in the original package.

But back to the topic at hand – it pleased God that He could cause all fullness to dwell in Christ. In other words, He rejoices just like those clowns when He sees the surprise on our faces and the delight in our hearts when we begin to experience the blessings that are ours in Christ – blessing that are more than we know how to contain (Malachi 3:10) and that are more than we could ever imagine or dare to ask for (Ephesians 3:20).

Day 3
No Void

Additionally, we must realize that Colossians 1:19 tells us at "all fullness dwells in Him." This means that there is no emptiness in Him. I think that many Christians seem to fail to grasp hold to this reality. A number of popular Christian songs, several faith-based movies, and at least one of the leading daily devotionals on the market today tout the idea that God is often distant, silent, or not responsive. The message that these compositions try to promote is the quality of patience, endurance, and trust during such times; however, they genuinely "miss the mark" in that they fail to recognize that He is a God who is ever present in our times of need (Psalm 46:1), that He is a friend that sticks closer than a brother (Proverbs 18:24), that He is Jehovah Shammah (Ezekiel 48:35) – the ever-present God who is always with us, even in the fiery furnace (Daniel 3:25). In Jesus, there is fullness – never void or emptiness.

> John bare witness of him, and cried, saying, This was he of whom I spake, He that cometh after me is preferred before me: for he was before me. And of his fulness have all we received, and grace for grace. (John 1:15-16)
>
> Which is his body, the fulness of him that filleth all in all. (Ephesians 1:23)
>
> And to know the love of Christ, which passeth knowledge, that ye might be filled with all the fulness of God. (Ephesians 3:19)
>
> For in him dwelleth all the fulness of the Godhead bodily. (Colossians 2:9)

Day 4
Salvation

Once we've opened the box and gotten over the recoil at all the treasures inside, the first package that we find inside is labeled "salvation." Second Timothy 2:10 assures us that we'll find salvation in Christ Jesus. Of course, that is the first and foremost selling point that gets most people to turn to the Jesus treasure chest in the first place. We are presented with the alternative that since we are sinners, we have only two options – either to accept Jesus and be saved or reject Him and go straight to hell without passing "Go" and receiving our two hundred dollars. In other word, Jesus is our "get out of hell free" card in life's grand Monopoly game.

I'm sure that we all remember the story of the thief on the cross who asked Jesus to remember him when He came into His kingdom (Luke 23:42), and we've all heard of the deathbed salvations or even the man on death row who prays with the chaplain just before walking that "long mile" to the gas chamber. These individuals have spent their whole lives living selfishly and in sin but turn to Jesus just before drawing their last breath. Of course, we rejoice that these individuals have received eternal life and will not, as the old Pentecostal preachers used to say, "split hell wide open." However, we must lament that they never got to explore all the riches were waiting for them in their Jesus treasure chest.

Jesus came that we could have abundant life here on earth – not just eternal life in heaven. In fact, John described eternal life not going to heaven but as knowing God, "This is life eternal, that they might know thee the only true God, and Jesus Christ, whom thou hast sent" (John 17:3) – digging into the treasure chest.

Day 5

Redemption

Along with salvation, we also receive redemption (Romans 3:24) – a treasure that illustrates an amazing aspect of God's love. I'd like to tell a little story about redemption. A young boy built a small model boat – a laborious task and labor of love. When he completed the project, he excitedly took his little vessel to the lake to test it out. Delighted, he watched as the wind filled the tiny sails and the boat began to gracefully cut through the waters. Unfortunately, a sudden gust of wind propelled the little boat just beyond his grasp. As he waded into the lake to retrieve the toy boat, the wind continued to push the boat further and further, until it disappeared. Heartbroken, the lad went home thinking that he might never see his little boat again; yet, one day, he was surprised to see it on display in the front window of a local pawn shop. Apparently, someone had found the boat and sold it to the store owner for a few pennies. When he rushed into the shop and told the sales clerk that the boat was his, the clerk's response was that it actually belonged to the store and the only way that the boy could have it would be to pay the asking price. When the lad broke his piggy bank, he discovered that it would take everything he had to pay for the little boat; however, he didn't hesitate to take every one of his coins – to the very last cent – to reclaim his treasured little boat. As he walked out of the pawn shop, he cuddled his prized little boat and exclaimed, "Now, you are twice mine – I made you, and I also bought you." That's the story of redemption – God made us, but bought us back at the terrible price of His own Son when we were lost due to our sins. Our salvation is actually a redemption – God's way of reclaiming us for His benefit – as well as a rescue.

Day 6

New Birth

Unless we understand the redemptive aspect of salvation, we run the risk of living our lives just like the deathbed converts – even though we may live for years or even decades after we receive salvation. Until we grasp this concept, we'll not understand how important it is to keep digging in the treasure chest – because it brings delight to Him as well as to us as we discover the jewels inside the box.

As we dig into our Jesus treasure chest, the next discovery we make is that we have new birth as well as salvation. Of course, it is easy to confuse the two because we often use the terms interchangeably; however, let's think back at our own lives and think about our salvation experience. We probably realized an immediate change in many areas.

In giving her testimony, my wife describes the night she was ready to commit suicide and "accidentally" picked up a piece of gospel literature that had been handed to her a few days earlier. After reading the tract and and praying the prayer on the last page, she fell asleep with the decision that she could postpone her suicide until the next morning. When she woke up the following dawn, she could hear the birds singing happier songs that she had ever remembered and see the sun shining a little brighter than she ever recollected. She had been born again as well as being saved. Had she already initiated her plan to take her own life before she prayed that prayer, she would have been saved and even redeemed – but because she gave the Lord a few more hours to work in her, she realized that she had actually become a new creature in Christ and that all the old aspects of her life had passed away as Paul described in II Corinthians 5:17.

Day 7

Suicide to the Old Man

In all reality, Peggy HAD committed suicide – she had crucified and mortified the old sinful woman she had been so that she could be reborn as a new righteous woman. (Colossians 3:5) In actuality, she had received two distinct gifts – salvation and the new birth as a new creature in Christ. Unfortunately, some people prefer to stop with just the first gift and never dig any deeper in the treasure chest to discover the wonderful gift that they have as new creatures in Christ.

But that is not the case here; we are excited about going deeper in Jesus – so let's keep digging into the chest. But before we pull out another gift, we realize that the "new birth" package we are holding seems pretty heavy. Maybe there is something inside. Yes, when we open it up, we discover that it is filled with many other gifts just waiting to be discovered. The first one that catches our eye is labeled "righteousness." Second Corinthians 5:21 records that we have been made the righteousness of God in Jesus. What a revelation! No matter how sinful our lives have been, we have been made totally righteous through the righteousness of Jesus who lived His full life without committing one sin. (Hebrews 4:15) As mysterious as it may seem that Jesus (who never sinned) was counted as being guilty of all our sins, it is equally unfathomable to conceive that we (who deserve no credit since all our good deeds are nothing more than polluted rags in God's sight) could be credited with all the righteousness of Jesus. Unthinkable? Yes! Impossible to comprehend? Yes! But true? Even more so, yes!!

Day 8

The Bonus Gift

Just as most products come with a warning that they be used properly and with the appropriate safety gear, this package comes with a user's manual notation that it is not to be abused as an excuse for sinning or a license to sin. (Galatians 5:13) In essence, this gift is our license to live free <u>from</u> sin rather than our permit to live freely <u>in</u> sin.

As we marvel at this incredible gift, we realize that it is actually a bonus package with another gift wrapped together with it. This second gift in the same wrapper is labeled "perfection" – a term that almost makes us cringe just to hear it, especially in relationship to our own lives since we all know our own selves well enough to know that our names and the term "perfection" don't legitimately belong in the same sentence. However, God says that in Christ, we have perfection and that it is His intent that we be presented as such. (Colossians 1:28) So what is perfection?

In the letter to the church at Sardis (Revelation 3:1-6), the Lord probed the question of perfection. It is commonly assumed that believers cannot obtain perfection and are, therefore, exempt from striving for it. In fact, that whole philosophy was once flaunted on bumper stickers that proclaimed, "Christians aren't perfect, just forgiven." Such a teaching ignored the testimonies of such biblical characters as Job (Job 1:1), Noah (Genesis 6:9), and Abraham (Genesis 17:1) as well as the words of Jesus Himself (Matthew 5:48, 19:21) and Paul's double admonition in Ephesians 4:11-13. The scriptural context of perfection seems to indicate that perfect people are ones whose actions are perfect because their hearts are perfect.

Day 9

Perfect Heart

The scriptures teach that Amaziah, for instance, did what was right but not with a perfect heart (II Chronicles 25:2). He apparently fell into the same category as the believers at Corinth who were doing good deeds – and even operating in spiritual gifts – yet their actions failed to be of benefit because they were not motivated by love. (I Corinthians 13:1-3) On the other hand, David was considered to be a man after God's own heart (Acts 13:22) even though he committed adultery and plotted the murder of the woman's husband. His prayer of repentance in the fifty-first Psalms explained why. His plea before God was that the Lord would not take the Holy Spirit from him and that He would renew a right heart within him. Apparently David understood the necessity of what Paul would later describe as the seal of the Holy Spirit (Ephesians 1:13, 4:30) – the quickening work of the Holy Spirit that constantly reminds the sensitive believer of the validity or lack thereof of his every thought, motive, and action. In spite of the fact that the focus of the letter is on those who do not have perfect works, the letter acknowledges that some believers do meet the acid test – and gracious promises are extended to them. (Ephesians 5:27, I John 3:3)

There were probably hundreds of young men on the road with the prodigal who could have used new robes and shoes; however, the father only sent his servants for one robe and one pair of shoes because there was only one young man on the road that day who had a heart relationship with him. Like our Heaven Father in I Chronicles 16:9, the prodigal's father was looking up and down the road, seeking for the son with a right heart toward him.

Day 10
Acceptance

But the "new birth" box is far from empty; so, let's see what we find next – acceptance. Romans 8:1 says that there is no condemnation when we are in Christ. This means that there is no reason for us to be rejected and every reason for us to be accepted. Well, we all know better than that. After all, we all remember our blunders – some accidental and some deliberately intentional. Certainly, if we have reason to condemn ourselves, God has even more. But this gift says that He doesn't find a reason to condemn us and accepts us anyway. Why? The answer can be found in the companion aspect of this gift – His unmerited favor (also known as grace). It has been said that mercy is not getting what we deserve whereas grace is getting what we don't deserve. Because of His mercy, God has determined not to cast us away from Himself for our sins; but, because of His grace, He has determined to bring us to Himself without having to earn the privilege. Paul admonished his protégé Timothy to be strong in the reality of this grace that he had in Christ Jesus. (II Timothy 2:1) In essence, understanding this unmerited favor that we have in Jesus should make us strong Christians who can demonstrate that we really are new creatures in Christ through grace, not weak ones who still think and act like the old unregenerate creatures we were before our new birth.

When Paul said in Ephesians 1:6 that we are accepted in the beloved, he used a term that appears only two times in the Bible – here and in Luke 1:28, where the angel Gabriel used this term to tell the Virgin Mary that she was "highly favored." In other words, our acceptance is not just a toleration; it is a full-blown celebration of our favored relationship in Christ.

Day 11

Life

Digging deeper into the "new birth" package, we find another gift labeled, "life." According to Romans 8:2, we traded in the law of sin and death for the law of life in Christ Jesus. This means that the very rule that determines our existence is one of life rather than one of death. Let me illustrate this point by sharing a little of the story from my mission work in Nepal. When I first became involved in ministry to Nepal, the country was recognized as the world's only Hindu kingdom, and the promotion of any other religion was strictly prohibited. There were Christians in the country, but they were there solely for humanitarian purposes. In order to have the privilege of staying in the country, they had to agree not to propagate their faith. The nationals who converted to Christianity did so at much peril, facing imprisonment, alienation from family and friends, loss of employment, and physical abuse and persecution. However, during the four years of intercession that led to my first physical ministry in the country, the king granted a new constitution to the people of the nation. One aspect of the new rule was religious freedom – meaning that I could go into the country and minster openly and freely. On one of my early trips, I was questioned about the huge boxes that were part of my luggage. I told the customs officers that they were filled with Christian literature in the Nepali language. I ripped one of the boxes open and started handing samples to all the men in the customs department. Had I been discovered bringing in such literature prior to the granting of the new constitution, I would have been sent to jail or deported, but now I was able to freely give the booklets to the very men who would formerly have been responsible to arrest me.

Day 12

Liberty

Allow me to continue with my experience in Nepal. Once I got into the country, I could freely stand on any public street and openly distribute my pamphlets. On one occasion when I was being literally mobbed by people wanting to get the free booklets, a police officer came up to see what was going on. When I told him what I was doing and showed him the literature, he responded that I was hindering traffic because of the huge crowd that had gathered. But instead of arresting me or telling me to stop, he asked for one of the boxes of tracts and started helping me pass them out so as to quickly disperse the crowd! This is a powerful example of what it means to move from one law to another. Previously, there was a law that incurred death, but now there was a law promoting life. So it is in Christ, we are translated from a legal system that results in death – dead works, spiritual death, and deadly thoughts and actions – into a new system that allows us to live and do works that bring life to others.

As we hold this glistening jewel of life up to the light, we see that it showers us with a spectrum of vivid colors, one of which illuminates another aspect of this gift – liberty. Just as my examples from my experience in Nepal have illustrated – moving into the law of life immediately gives us liberty. Prior to the new law, I did not have liberty to bring gospel literature into the nation. In fact, one of my friends spent time in a Nepali prison because the customs officers – and I've often wondered if they might have been the same ones to whom I gave the gospel tracts – discovered Bibles in his luggage when entering the country prior to the implementation of the new constitution.

Day 13

Good Lives

Again, this package comes with a safety warning that we always use our liberty in Christ to promote life rather than to allow it to become a source of bondage through abuse or misrepresentation. (Galatians 2:4)

Associated with the new persons that we have been fashioned into in Christ is the fact that we are given the liberty to live good lives. The Apostle Peter speaks of this reality when he says that we have good "conversation" in Christ in I Peter 3:16 – and old term that today would be translated "lifestyle." The liberty that we have in Christ is not anarchy – the rejection of moral obligation. Rather it is the freedom to totally embrace moral obligation and to live lives that hallmark graciousness, honesty, and nobility.

Along with this good life that we have in Christ come promises. (Ephesians 3:6) A little later on in the same context, Paul spoke of the things that God was working in us as being more than we could ever imagine or dare to ask for (Ephesians 3:20) – yet, they are all promised to us. Jesus described this in parabolic form when He likened the Heavenly Father to human fathers and illustrated how we humans will do all in our power to ensure that we give our children the best we can afford. Then He surprised His audience by saying that even in doing so graciously, we are still evil. In contrast, God – in whom there is not even a glimmer of evil – gives us even more great and precious promises. (II Peter 1:4) Paul used the terminology of the passing on of an inheritance to an adopted son to make the same point; however, we may often fail to grasp the full meaning of his illustration because we don't know the biblical background of adoption – an idea that we will explore tomorrow.

Day 14

Adoption, Inheritance, and Victory

The practice of adoption in biblical times was one of providing an avenue of passing on an inheritance. If a man had no son, he would usually adopt a nephew to become his heir. This practice kept the wealth inside the family rather than letting it be lost to outsiders. Notice in the story of Abraham and Lot that it was only after Lot had separated from Abraham (Genesis 13:14) that Abraham became concerned about the fact that he had no heir (verse 15:2). Unlike adoption today, which may be based on sympathy for orphaned children or the loneliness of childless couples, the adoption mentioned here was based solely on the desire to pass on benefits. If we see our position in Christ in this light, we will understand that God is not intending that this benefit to be jeopardized. He wants to make an investment in us, and He does not intend to see that investment stolen or destroyed.

But the '"new birth" box is still far from empty. There is another package that catches our attention – victory. Paul boasted in II Corinthians 2:14 that the Lord always causes us to triumph in Christ. That means that if we are in Christ, we can and should experience perpetual victory. In Colossians 2:15, Paul adds, "And having spoiled principalities and powers, he made a shew of them openly, triumphing over them in it." The literal meaning of "spoiled" is "stripped him naked." The verse is actually rendered this way in some modern translations, vividly reiterating the scene being set here. The imagery behind this wording comes from the ancient practice of defrocking the kings and other political and military leaders of conquered nations, but we must wait until tomorrow to fully unpack this truth.

Day 15
Magnificence

When defeated enemies were brought back from the battle, they were totally humiliated by being marched through the streets naked – no longer with royal robes or regalia of rank. Through the wording he used to speak our victorious position and the devil's defeated position, Paul painted a vivid picture to awaken his reader to the fact that the opponent against whom we are to stand is an already defeated foe. In Christ, we always stand in this kind of victory.

Another gleaming package in our chest is labeled "magnificence." According to Ephesians 2:10, we are the workmanship of God created in Christ Jesus. Of course, it is exciting enough to realize that we are God's handiwork rather than just the result of a long series of evolutionary accidents that traces our ancestry through monkeys to pond scum. However – as mind boggling as that revelation may be – this is just a scratch on the surface or a drop in the ocean compared to what Paul was really trying to say. The word that he used in this verse actually means that we are more than just God's handicrafts; we are His masterpieces. In other words, we are his "Mona Lisa"s and His "Michelangelo's David"s. Yes, there have been millions of paintings of pretty women and statues of handsome men – and all of them are unique and worthy of appreciation because they are the handiwork of talented artisans. However, there is only one Mona Lisa and only one David; they are the masterpieces of genius artists. If Leonardo da Vinci and Michelangelo could produce such magnificent works of art that capture the awe and respect of not only art lovers and critics, but of the common man as well – imagine what it means that you are God's masterpiece.

Day 16

Enlightenment

For certain, we have not come anywhere near to emptying the "new birth" treasure trove; so, let's get back to digging deeper into the Jesus treasure chest. As we turn our attention back to the bigger box, we come across another parcel labeled "enlightenment" – an aspect that the Apostle John considered so significant that he presented it prominently in the introductory section to his gospel. (John 1:4) In one of his epistles, the beloved disciple came back to this same idea but approached it from the opposite direction by saying that we would be free from deception because there is no darkness at all in Christ. (I John 1:5) Paul explained that we can now have perfect clarity concerning the things of God with his comment that the veil that has kept men from understanding the truth has been taken away in Christ. (II Corinthians 3:14)

What this package ensures is that we can now understand what all the packages that we have been pulling out of the "new birth" box really are and how they actually function. In what is probably the most powerful apostolic prayer, Paul interceded for the saints in Ephesus, "That the God of our Lord Jesus Christ, the Father of glory, may give unto you the spirit of wisdom and revelation in the knowledge of him: The eyes of your understanding being enlightened; that ye may know what is the hope of his calling, and what the riches of the glory of his inheritance in the saints, And what is the exceeding greatness of his power to us-ward who believe, according to the working of his mighty power, Which he wrought in Christ, when he raised him from the dead, and set him at his own right hand in the heavenly places." (Ephesians 1:17-20)

Day 17

Cheese and Crackers

A little story from the glory days of Ellis Island and the influx of immigrants into our nation tells about a man who saved every penny he could get his hands on to book passage on a steamer across the Atlantic so that he could start a new life in America. Once he had enough money to pay for his ticket, he took the remaining few coins he had to buy a wheel of cheese and a big tin of crackers. Each morning when the other passengers gathered for a scrumptious breakfast, he retreated to his berth and opened his tin and made himself a meal of cheese and crackers. At noon each day, he enviously eyed his fellow shipmates as they headed again to the dining hall for their lunch. Again, he slipped into his bunk and nourished himself with cheese and crackers. Most tragically of all, his mouth would water as he saw the banquet spread every night for dinner – but, alas, his meal was again cheese and crackers. It was only on the last day of his voyage across the mighty ocean that someone showed him that his ticket read, "All meals included." As heartrending as this story may be, it is even more sobering to realize that it is being played out every day in the lives of millions of Christians around the world who simply haven't dug deeply enough into their Jesus treasure chest to see that their salvation is more than a ticket to a new life in heaven – that it is also an all-inclusive program while they are on the journey. But in Christ, there is the promise that we can know what we actually already own and can understand how to activate those possessions, privileges, and promises.

Day 18
The Love Package

I can't imagine the surprise that ricochets through our emotions as we reach in to pull out the next package and discover that it is labeled "love." In that love is the basic definition of our relationship with God and even His own personality (I John 4:7-8), it's hard to imagine why this package was buried so far down in the chest. Speaking of the love that we have in Christ, the Apostle Paul says that there is nothing that can separate us from it: not life, not death, not angels, not demons, not things from the present, not things of the future, not things that are high, not things that low – nothing! (Romans 8:39) In light of this passage, it is understandable that we may not really understand what God's love is actually about until we have experienced it in times of difficulty. When I first started going to Nepal, it was just coming out of years of persecution of Christians; therefore, I had the privilege of getting to know many individuals who had endured much for Jesus' sake. One such woman was the lady who always found a place on the front row in every service at the church in Kathmandu. Her face was so horribly distorted and disfigured that I decided to ask the pastor about her story. His answer shocked me. When her Hindu husband discovered that she was attending Christian services, he threw battery acid in her face! In spite of the pain and suffering, in spite of the permanent disfiguration, in spite of the humiliation, in spite of everything that could have turned her into a bitter, unforgiving, recluse – she was warm and loving, she was joyful and jubilant, she danced and clapped more excitedly than almost anyone else. The love of God erupted from her – the result of her having dug deeply into the Jesus treasure chest.

Day 19

Consolation

The flip side of the love that we find in Christ is that we also find consolation in Him. (Philippians 2:1) This is the comfort that comes with resting in His love in spite of the challenges that accompany our decision to follow Him. Let me take you to the African nation of Niger to get a picture of what this means. I want you to meet my good friend in the capital city who hosts me when I come to this country which is ninety-eight percent Muslim. As a fourteen-year-old boy, he heard and received the Good News of Jesus Christ. Well, it was good news to him, but bad news to his strict Muslim parents. No matter how much they tried to convince him to recant, they could not dissuade his new faith. Finally, they did the only thing left to preserve their honor in the community – they disowned their son, declared him dead, and expelled him from their home. Now, barely into his teens, this young man had to find a way to support himself in the crowded city of Niamey. Knowing that no one would give him food or shelter because he had brought shame upon his family by becoming an "infidel," he knew of only one place to turn – the American missionary who had introduced him to Christ. The missionary had little to offer, but he gave the young boy a place to stay and food in exchange for his services in cleaning his house. This is where the consolation comes in – rather than moping about feeling sorry for himself, my friend modeled himself after Joseph who found himself as a slave and later a prisoner in Egypt. He joyfully cleaned the missionary's house and threw himself into every opportunity he could to learn more and more about his new faith – he wanted to go deeper in Jesus, if you will. And tomorrow, we'll learn the rest of his story.

Day 20

Blessing

Because my friend in Niger focused on the consolation that he found in Christ, he wanted to know more than what was written in the few books translated into his local dialect; therefore, he learned French (the official language of his region) and then turned to English (the missionary's native tongue). The end result was that by the time he was in his early twenties, he was able to do international business and make a comfortable living – something that would never have happened had he stayed in his father's home or even if he had taken the room with the missionary but done so without letting God give him consolation in Christ.

Reaching into our treasure chest again, we pull out another glistening package – this one labeled "blessing." The Apostle Paul encouraged us that we have all spiritual blessings in Christ. (Ephesians 1:3) Let me share a lesson from the Greek language concerning the word "all." It means exactly the same thing in Greek that it does in English – all, every, nothing excluded! I know that it is so easy for us to categorize the blessings of God and feel that certain things belong to certain superheroes of the faith. Yes, we believe that Oral Roberts or Billy Graham can have all sorts of blessings because they are Oral Roberts and Billy Graham; therefore, they are in a totally different category from us and we shouldn't think that such things could ever be ours. Well, have you ever stopped to think of the logic – or, actually, the lack of logic – in that argument? It is not being Oral Roberts or Billy Graham that invokes the blessing; it is the blessing that made Oral Roberts and Billy Graham the men they are in the ministry. The blessings are in Christ – not in the recognized ministers.

Day 21

Miraculous Rain

Come with me, if you will, to the island nation of Sri Lanka to see an illustration of the point that blessings belong to all of us – not just Billy Graham or Oral Roberts. A number of years ago, my wife and I arrived in the country to minister in a youth camp that had been arranged for the Christian high school and college students in that Buddhist state. When our host picked us up at the airport, he announced that we were going to have to cancel the retreat. He then went on to explain that the country was encountering a severe drought and that there was no water in the cisterns at the retreat center. Without water for cooking, cleaning, and washing, it would be impossible to house the group at the camp. I explained that we had spent a lot of money in advance to cover the camp expenses and had flown all the way from America for the event. In my mind, it was impossible to cancel the retreat. There had to be a way to make it work. I asked for just twenty-four hours before he made his final decision. That night we asked the Lord for the windows of heaven to be opened in some miraculous way, and God answered our prayer in an even more dramatic way than I had anticipated. We had the most horrendous rainstorm I have ever experienced. It didn't just "rain cats and dogs"; it was more like lions and wolves. I had never seen anything like it; the rain came down by the buckets full – no, barrels full. Not only did the cisterns fill to overflowing, the drought that was crippling the nation's agriculture was immediately alleviated. As a result, we were able to go forward with our plans for the retreat where we saw many young lives changed and destinies set. But the story doesn't end there! I'll share the rest tomorrow.

Day 22
Simplicity

It wasn't until I revisited the Sri Lanka almost thirty years later and was asked by one of the prominent pastors of the country to preach in his church that I saw proof of the remaining effect of the night that the windows of heaven were opened. That pastor who is now a significant leader in the country was called into the ministry as a high school student in that camp that would have been canceled had God not opened the windows of heaven.

My point in telling this story is that it didn't take Oral Roberts or Billy Graham to bring the rain that night – the blessing was in Christ, not in any minister, and I could access it as readily as Oral Roberts or Billy Graham could have. And so can you – if you decide to go deeper in Jesus and keep looking into your Jesus treasure chest.

As we have seen with many of the packages we've opened so far, there is often a flip side to the package. And such is the case here. The back side of the blessing package is labeled, "simplicity" – a corrective to overindulgence or misdirection of the blessings that we have in Christ. Paul actually used the word "fear" when he spoke of his concern that the believers could be enticed to abandon the simplicity that is in Christ. (II Corinthians 11:3) But before we go too far in this discussion, it is necessary that we understand that "simplicity" does not mean "depravity." Unfortunately, many Christians think that living in simplicity means that they give up all the niceties of life in order to be godly. There are several problems with that mentality, which we will examine over the next couple days.

Day 23

Wrong Images of God

The first misconception is that it prompts is a wrong image of God – one that portrays Him as barely having enough to go around. Yes, it's wrong and unchristian to take a second helping when there are others who haven't had their first helping, but the truth is that our God is El Shaddia, the God who has more than enough so that everyone can have seconds! We need to develop a both-and rather than an either-or mentality about the blessings of God. Let me take you to a behind-the-scenes meeting among several ministers who were working on a project to raise money for a humanitarian program to feed orphaned children in Africa. When one of the men reached across the table to take a roll from the bread basket, his sleeve pulled up enough to reveal his expensive high-end watch. Another one of the ministers at the table commented, "Just think how many children we could have fed with what it cost to buy that watch." The first gentleman responded, "You have no idea how many children I fed before I bought this watch." You see, there was no error in having the watch because he did not defraud anyone out of a meal in order to get it.

A second error that results from the simplicity-depravity confusion is the subjective evaluation of blessing. Had the first gentleman's watch been of the same price range as the second gentleman's timepiece, the discussion would never have occurred. The point that we need to understand is that we cannot subjectively set the standard for defining blessings; we must go by the objective standard that God has already set. And that is that He wants to pour out (not just sprinkle) blessings on us to the point the we cannot physically contain them. (Malachi 3:10)

Day 24

Lavish

In Ephesians 1:8, Paul speaks of wisdom and prudence that He made to abound toward us. The New International Version translates this clause, "He has lavished upon us." One fast-food restaurant puts the meat on a scale to make sure that the customer gets exactly the right number of ounces. If the scale tips a little high, the counter attendant tears off a little so that the customer gets exactly the amount he pays for – and not a bit more. "Lavish," on the other hand, means that there is no scale. God's blessings are spread out for us like an all-you-can-eat buffet. "Lavish" actually implies an over-the-top excess – like the world-record-breaking three-hundred-thirty-eight-pound burger produced at Mallie's Sports Grill and Bar in Southgate, Michigan; it was three feet high, had more than half a million calories, and took twenty-two hours to cook. Why did Mallie's make such a monster of a hamburger? Because they could. Why does God lavish His blessing upon us? Because He can. We serve a God named El Shaddai, the God of More Than Enough. He lavishly gives us abundance, "good measure, pressed down, and shaken together, and running over." (Luke 6:38)

One other point that we should understand in regard to this concept is that it promotes a mentality that actually makes the devil look more generous that God when we see non-Christians enjoying prosperity that we Christians have deprived ourselves of in the attempt to be simplistic. King Solomon didn't ask for wealth, but God placed more than the top four hundred present-day billionaires combined into his lap! His wealth made him the envy of pagan kings instead of the other way around.

Day 25
Satisfaction in Our Relationship with Jesus

Having said all this, now it is time to actually define what the simplicity that we have in Christ really is. It is a heart attitude in which we realize that our real satisfaction is in our relationship with Christ – not in complicated theological explanations about Him or in what He has given to us. One of the greatest influences that I have had in my life was Dr. Lester Sumrall, one of the great Christian authors, broadcasters, missionaries, and pastors of the last century. Due to our deeply personal relationship, I often found myself in private personal prayer time with him. Let me reiterate exactly who this man was. He was the pastor of a three-thousand member church, the author of over one hundred publications, the founder of a Christian educational system that covered all the bases from daycare to doctoral degrees, the president of a broadcasting system that owned a dozen television stations and five shortwave radio stations that literally blanketed the globe with the gospel, director of a world-wide humanitarian program that operated two cargo ships and a cargo plane to bring food, medical supplies, and the gospel to every continent in the world – and the list could go on and on. Now back to the prayer room – I will never forget his earnest prayer, "Lord, I want to know you." Even after more than sixty years in active full-time ministry, he was still wanting to go deeper in Jesus and dig further down into His treasure chest! There was no shortage of blessings – he handled millions of dollars each year – but his simplicity was in his relationship with the God of the blessings, not the blessings of God. That's the simplicity that we must have to balance out the abundance that we have in Christ.

Day 26

Confidence

Well, what have we here? The next item that I've snared in my treasure chest is marked as "confidence." First John 6:14 assures us that we have confidence in Christ that all our prayers will be answered when we pray according to His will. This confidence is not because of our great ability to fashion eloquent prayers that impress or convince God with our mastery of the art of praying. Neither does it come from our ability to force God's hand through our sincerity or earnestness in moaning, groaning, staining our voices, or starving ourselves through fasting. No, the confidence that we find in our treasure chest is simply because all the promises of God are guaranteed in Christ. Paul emphasized that they are doubly sure when he proclaimed that they are yea and amen – certainty to the second power! (II Corinthians 1:20)

Have you ever had the experience of having to find a store that was open on Christmas morning to buy the batteries that you failed to get to go along with the "batteries not included" toys that you just presented to your children? At our house, there is a standing joke that I give all my sons – and now my grandsons – a package of batteries every Christmas even if they don't get gifts that require them. Well, when we pull out the next package from our chest, we discover that it is labeled "faith" – exactly the gift that we need to activate the previous gift of confidence in the divine guarantees that are in Christ. Paul spoke of the Colossians believers as being steadfast in the faith that they had in Christ (Colossians 2:5) and of the abundance of faith that Timothy had in Christ (I Timothy 1:14) – the empowering aspects of faith that takes us beyond just wishful thinking, pipe dreams, and hopeful dream.

Day 27
The Walnut Tree – Part I

Some of my favorite stories on the topic of confidence have to do with giving in faith for missions.

While I was dean of the Bible college in Indiana, in the backyard of our home stood a giant walnut tree whose upper limbs brushed the very heavens. It was the home of a multitude of grey squirrels that scampered up and down its trunk and ducked into its hollow knotholes only to reappear on the other side of the tree ten feet further down the tree's trunk. This disappearance and reappearance of the furry little creatures became a little discomforting to us since it meant that the tree must be hollow for some major section of its trunk. Since the tree leaned across the roof of our house, we began to feel that it endangered our home and our lives if it were to be blown over. Several severe storms took their toll of limbs from other trees in our yard; yet the giant walnut remained intact even though it rocked and creaked with the violent winds. I talked to several companies about removing the tree but was constantly offered bids that were far beyond my price range. One friend of mine who did tree removal as a sideline volunteered to take it down for us as a favor. But, after climbing the tree and surveying how much actually reached over the house, he descended and rescinded. We tried to postpone the removal until a later date when we might have the extra cash to pay for the service. But when a violent windstorm raged through our area bringing down one of the trees in our yard, my wife insisted that we act immediately before the next storm razed the walnut that, in turn, would crush our home.

And tomorrow, we'll see what this walnut tree has to do with confidence in God's promises.

Day 28

The Walnut Tree – Part II

Since the next week was our annual campmeeting and I knew that I would be busy morning, noon, and night, I promised, without fail, to call a tree company immediately after the conference. In one of the sessions, Dr. Sumrall took a special offering for missions, and I responded by making a five-hundred-dollar donation on my credit card. Now, this was a real step of faith because I knew that I would have to pay around eight hundred dollars to get the tree removed the following week. Now, I was adding an additional obligation of five hundred more dollars. Where would I get an extra thirteen hundred dollars before the end of the month? I had no idea, but I had confidence that I had to obey the Lord on the missions offering and my wife on the tree removal.

When I went home for lunch after the service in which I had made the missions pledge, I found a stranger standing in my backyard. I went to find out what he wanted and was greeted with a proposal that I sell him the walnut lumber from the tree. He had been in the area for some other wood procurement and had spotted this tree towering on the skyline. It seemed ideal for his veneer business and he was willing to pay five hundred dollars for it. I quickly settled the deal and arranged for free removal – saving me the eight hundred dollars that it would have cost me to have a tree removal company take it down. I also pocketed the five-hundred-dollar check and used it to pay off my missions pledge. I'm still amazed at how that the man was driving in my neighborhood and showed up in my backyard on the very day that I planted a missionary seed. Not only that – he offered me the exact amount that I had given in the offering!

Day 29

More Confidence Stories

As a college student, I organized my funds by taking my monthly check and dividing my spending money into four envelopes – one for each week. One night at a special missions rally, I felt impressed to empty my wallet for the offering. This left me a full week behind on my finances, but when I opened my envelope for the next week – much to my surprise – there was twice as much as I had put there! Another experience while I was in college was when I felt directed to empty my wallet in a missionary offering one Friday evening. I knew that that meant I would be penniless until the next weekend, but I also knew that my God would somehow take care of me. When I got back to the dorm that night, there was a note on my door directing me to call one of the college professors that night – no matter how late it was that I got in. Even though I hated to call at a rather late hour, I knew that there was an urgency behind the professor's message; so, I returned his call. He greeted me with the offer to work for him the next day. He had received an opportunity to do some side work and needed an assistant – work that I knew how to help him with. Of course, I agreed and met him early the next morning for a full day's work. At the end of the day, he paid me in cash – more than I had put in the offering the night before. That missionary seed brought me an immediate harvest! Not only that – the business opportunity continued for the professor, and he employed me week after week for a number of months, greatly multiplying the seed I had sown.

Day 30
Authority and Anointing

Along with faith come two other powerful evidences of what we have in Christ – authority and anointing. Revelation 1:6 informs us that we are in the position of kings and priests in Christ and that dominion or authority has been attributed to Him. The only logical conclusion is that this authority is to be executed through His ordained officials – meaning us! The beloved disciple assures us that there is an anointing that we received in Christ and that this anointing abides – or is readily available – in us at all times. (I John 2:27) So, how do this authority and anointing function? To illustrate the point, let's look at a few testimonies of encounters with demonic forces that really drew upon the gift of faith and the authority and anointing birthed from it.

It was a dark and stormy night – well, actually it wasn't stormy, and it wasn't any darker than any other ordinary night. But the events of that evening seem to fit so perfectly into one of those "dark and stormy night" stories that I just couldn't resist the intro line. I was visiting the University of North Carolina's Wilmington campus. Since it was only a few miles from Wrightsville Beach, our group had decided to stay with a friend who managed an old beachfront hotel on the Atlantic Coast. The old building had long since seen its better days and was soon to be bulldozed down to make way for the parking lot for a modern condominium. After checking into our rooms, we headed back to town for a Bible study on the campus. About halfway through the study, a young lady sort of floated into the room. With an out-of-this-world daze in her eye, she looked around and asked, "What is this place?" And over the next couple stormy nights – or mornings – we'll see what happened next.

Day 31

The Occult Books

We responded that it was a Bible study and that she was welcome to sit down and join us. Her reply was that she was just walking down the hall when "the spirit" told her to come in, so she took a seat and glared around the room as we completed our session. After the meeting, several of the students talked and prayed with her until it was time to leave the room. At that point, one of the students who was traveling with me suggested that our guest come back to the hotel with us for some further counseling. She decided to accept the invitation, and we headed for the beach. As soon as we parked, I began to feel the uncanny sensation that I was walking into a horror movie. The eeriness continued to mount as we entered the back door. Inside, the kitchen was vibrant with an unearthly presence. On the table we found a large box with a note attached. It was from a young man who had just received Jesus into his heart that day. It explained that, with his new life, he wanted to totally break from the old one that had involved a lot of occultism. The box contained all his occult books that he wished to destroy but was afraid to do by himself. His request was that we burn them for him. Eager to rid the house of the unholy manifestation, we grabbed the box and headed for the fireplace. In that it was winter and that this relic of a hotel was anything but airtight, a roaring fire was already waiting for us in the lobby. All the lobby furniture was huddled around the fireplace as a resort for all the guests as we tried to defend ourselves against the chilly ocean breezes that blew almost as freely through the hotel as they did on the windswept sand dunes outside. Our group, including the new guest, grabbed seats close to the open fireplace as we began to toss the occult books into the flames.

Day 32
The Deliverance

Our new friend, in an almost hypnotic voice, began to talk about each of the books as she pulled them out of the box, "This is an expensive book; we can't burn it. This is a nice one; why do you want to destroy it?" We all knew that something was wrong, but no one knew what to do or say. Upon our insistence, every book made it to the inferno, but the evil presence remained. It was at that point that we realized that the demon was not in the books but in the co-ed from the campus – so we began to cast it out. None of us had ever done that before, so we were novices using the trial-and-error method. At one point, we asked the young lady if she wanted Jesus to come into her heart so that she could go to heaven; the response was, "Oh, heaven will be boring – just sitting around playing a harp." At that instant, I realized that I had not been talking to the young lady at all, but that my conversation was with a demon that was speaking through her. I demanded that the spirit be quiet so that the girl could hear and respond. Calling her name, I commanded her to answer me and to receive Jesus into her heart and join me in commanding the demon to leave. She did – and she was free. No longer did she stare with hollow eyes into space. No longer did she speak in a monotone. No longer did she move catatonically. Suddenly she was a vibrant, vivacious young girl. But, she had one major problem – she didn't know where she was or how she had gotten there. Looking at her watch, she exclaimed, "How did it get this late? I've only been gone about ten minutes!" In actuality, she had been in the hotel lobby at least two hours plus all the time she was in the classroom on campus. The spirit that had been controlling her had actually obliterated all reality out of her consciousness.

Day 33
Authority and Anointing Against Demons

Since that day at Wrightsville Beach, I have met many others under the devil's control and have seen them set free in the name of Jesus. When I rebuked the spirit in one man who came to my office for prayer, the demon threw him across the room, and he crashed into the wall. When he picked himself up, he began to hop around the room like a frog as his mouth began to spew out the vilest forms of blasphemy and profanity. Yet, at the name of Jesus, he was instantly free and stood to his feet a new man. When he came back for follow-up counseling the next day, he stopped at the receptionist's desk and asked to see me. The receptionist called me to inform me that a gentleman claiming to be the one who had been in the prior day was there for an appointment. She added, "But this isn't the same man; I've never seen this man before." He was so radically changed that it showed on his face.

Another young man came to me for counseling and prayer. Under terrible bondage of low self-esteem, he refused to look up. Recognizing this as a demonic torment, I put my hand under his chin and forced him to raise his head and look me straight in the eyes. After ministering deliverance to him, I took him with me to a Christian fellowship meeting. Before long, people who had known the lad for several months began to come up and welcome the "newcomer" to the group. They had never seen him with his head up and did not recognize him as the same person they had known for a number of weeks.

These changed lives were possible because I had found authority and anointing in my Jesus treasure chest. "Behold, I give unto you power to tread on serpents and scorpions, and over all the power of the enemy." (Luke 10:19)

Day 34

Why Am I Here?

Well, let's get back to digging into our Jesus treasure chest. First, let's take a breather and set the stage for our next jewel. All of us want to fulfill our destiny. Each of us has asked the questions, "Why am I here?" and "What is my purpose?" We are all born with a sense of purpose and the feeling that there is a reason for our being on the earth. I am certain that even atheists and evolutionists share these same feelings even though they refuse to acknowledge the fact that there is a Master Designer behind everything and that He gives purpose to the lives of human beings. In fact, He gives purpose to everything, whether human or not, whether animate or inanimate. Just try to find anything in the created order that does not serve a significant function. Even the evolutionists who claim to believe that everything is nothing more than the result of one very long string of random accidents will fight to preserve every species of toads no matter how insignificant and every ecosystem no matter how remote. Why? Because they believe that every aspect of nature is vital to the rest of our environment. They would never admit that these very feelings contradict and disprove the very foundational premises of their philosophy. If they are correct in their theory that life as we know it today is the result of a series of unorchestrated events, then most of what we see in the world would be the leftovers from the failed trials. To prove this theory, all we have to do is visit any craftsman's workshop. One of the prominent fixtures will be a trash bin where he tosses all the imperfect specimens, scraps from his projects, and his failed attempts. There is probably more refuse going out the backdoor than sellable product going out the front door.

Day 35
From Microcosm to Macrocosm

Now, if we apply yesterday's illustration from the microcosm of a workshop to the macrocosm of the earth, the logical conclusion would be that only a minor portion of what exists in the earth today is significant and valuable – an assumption that would lead us to exploit and pollute with no concern for the consequences. Yes, that is exactly the mindset that once dominated our thinking. But we have since learned that the South American rainforest must be preserved if we hope to sustain life elsewhere on the planet. We have learned that every living creature – from aardvarks to zebras – serves a vital role somewhere in a chain that supports the entire livelihood of the planet. As the old saying goes, a chain is only as strong as its weakest link. Today, we realize how important every link is and we all go to any length to strengthen every one because we see how vital each one is to the whole. Amazingly, the crusaders who campaign the strongest are those who refuse to admit that such a delicate interdependence could only be the result of the work of a deliberate, intelligent Designer! If their theory that everything is the result of random accidental chance were true, then most of what they are so adamantly protecting is actually nothing more than the sawdust on the floor and the refuse in the waste bin and dumpster rather than the actual crafted masterpiece of the craftsman.

I said all that simply to say this – we have a tendency to treat the owls, whales, and rainforests as if they are significant parts of a grand masterpiece even when we don't acknowledge that there is a Master Creator behind them all.

Day 36

Lifetime Purpose

Once we acknowledge that there is a Creator at work, the whole process becomes logical and more significant. At this point, we must ask ourselves if the Creator gave significance to the aardvarks and the tree toads, certainly He had a purpose for each of the humans He created – and there is more to that purpose than just working in a factory or office all week and drinking beer in front of the football game on television.

The Apostle Paul wrote that he had been separated from his mother's womb for the assignment that Jesus gave him on the road to Damascus. Now, that is a pretty radical idea – especially when we realize that it was probably more than three decades between these two events and that Saul had worked harder than any of his contemporaries trying to do exactly the opposite of what Jesus had planned for him. Our first introduction to Paul is as Saul of Tarsus, a persecutor of the early Christians. He grew up as a freeborn Roman citizen in the city of Tarsus, which he called "no mean city," indicating that it was far above the average city of his time. It was certainly no average place in that it was a major center of commerce, education, and military power. With the excellent education that his writings demonstrate that Paul possessed and his Roman privilege coupled with the strong ethic his Jewish upbringing afforded him, Paul would have been a success in any field he would have chosen to pursue: business, military, academics, etc. Yet, he chose to abandon any of these lucrative pursuits and give himself to the study of theology at the rabbinic school of Gamaliel in Jerusalem, a career that rendered him so little financial security that he had to augment his livelihood by making tents.

Day 37
Misdirected Purpose

The biblical records indicate that Saul was bothered by anything that deviated from the theological doctrines he had learned in the synagogue and the rabbinical school; that's why he was persecuting the church. (Acts 9:2) He was adamant that the Christian movement – which he considered to be a blasphemous perversion of the Jewish faith – be crushed to death before it had a chance to spread its infectious heresy any further. As a personal disciple of Gamaliel, Saul gained an excellent command of biblical and traditional knowledge and the expertise to expound on these concepts, and it is also likely that he gained influence in the Jewish community through his association with the prominent rabbi and Sanhedrin member. (Acts 5:34)

It was probably this association that afforded him access to the high priest who granted him papers to go to Damascus in his attempt to eliminate the Christian faith before it penetrated this pivotal city. (Acts 9:2) Damascus was a terminal and transit point for all the major trade routes of the time – the frankincense route coming out of the Arabian Peninsula, the gold route coming out of Africa, and the silk route coming out of the Far East – all connecting to the Roman highway system that brought these goods to the capital of the world. Saul knew that if this new religion were able to become entrenched in the city of Damascus it would soon spread like a contagious disease along these corridors of commerce until it had infected the entire known world. Thus, he used his influence, connections, and eloquence to gain permission to implement his strategic plan to excise this religious "cancer" before it entered the bloodstream of the society.

Day 38

The Road to Damascus

It was on his campaign to eradicate Christianity in Damascus that Saul encountered Jesus and was converted to the faith that he was so adamantly persecuting and attempting to eradicate. Acts chapter nine describes the dramatic encounter in which Saul was knocked to the ground and blinded by the brilliant light that emanated from the Risen Christ. Those with him were also impacted by the encounter but did not hear the words that Jesus spoke to His captive that day, "Saul, Saul, why persecutest thou me? I am Jesus whom thou persecutest: it is hard for thee to kick against the pricks. Arise, and go into the city, and it shall be told thee what thou must do." (Acts 9:4-6) With the help of his companions, the blinded crusader found his way to a home on the main street of the city of Damascus. After three days of fasting and soul searching, Saul's conversion was completed when the Lord sent a reluctant evangelist to find him. When the Lord spoke to Ananias, he immediately refused with the logical objection that Saul's only motive for being in Damascus was to arrest Christians – and Ananias could think of a whole lot of better things to do that day than to walk directly into such a trap. The Lord continued to deal with His messenger, telling him that He had already shown Paul a vision of a man by the specific name of Ananias coming to him. With that kind of preannouncement before the Lord even spoke to him about the assignment, Ananias decided that there really wasn't an alternative. Through Ananias' ministry that day, Saul was healed, baptized in water, and filled with the Holy Spirit. Additionally, Ananias was able to speak into Paul's life concerning the Lord's will for his future. (Acts 9:15-16)

Day 39

Foreordained Purpose

It seems that Paul's predetermined destiny is not unique but that this lifelong purpose is universal. "According as he hath chosen us in him before the foundation of the world, that we should be holy and without blame before him in love: Having predestinated us unto the adoption of children by Jesus Christ to himself, according to the good pleasure of his will, To the praise of the glory of his grace, wherein he hath made us accepted in the beloved." (Ephesians 1:4-6)

Yes, Paul was a man who was destined by God to become His apostle and servant. But, he emphatically proclaimed that the same provision has been made for every believer. God has been working a plan for all of our lives – even from before the foundation of the world. As I was growing up, I always enjoyed reading the World Book Encyclopedia and National Geographic Magazine. I always took a lot of ribbing about wanting to stay inside and read when I could have been outside playing. Now, don't get me wrong – I did enjoy playing outside, riding bikes, building tree houses and forts in the woods behind our house, and chasing the neighborhood girls out of our backyard – but I also loved to read about other places in the world and about the cultures and religions of the people who lived there. It wasn't until I was an adult that I realized that all that reading was God's way of preparing me for a lifetime of cross-cultural missions work around the world. I believe that God preordained a path for my life and designed my temperament and interests so that I would be perfectly fitted for the job – He gave me an interest in the world so that I could go to His disciples around the globe and encourage them in their faith.

Day 40
Finding Destiny

And if He did it for me, I'm totally convinced that He's done it for you as well. Therefore, if you are asking those universal questions about your destiny, I suggest that you simply look at who you are because the Lord fashioned you specifically for your unique destiny. Is there something that you are specifically good at? Where do you think that talent came from? God, of course – and He gave it to you so that you could fulfill a specific calling that could never be accomplished without that ability.

As we have seen, Paul had great giftings that could have propelled him far in life; however, he came to realize that the will of God for him was to serve in the role of an apostle. (I Corinthians 1:1, II Corinthians 1:1, Ephesians 1:1, Colossians 1:1, II Timothy 1:1) He learned the lesson that we all must remember – God's call on your life is a heavenly GPS, giving you a locater of where you are and where you are to go in life.

I think of a couple of the greatest musicians in American history who, as young men, said that they had been called to preach the gospel. Unfortunately, they decided to pursue secular careers with the gift of music that God had given them as part of the ministry that He had intended for them to pursue. Both men made great fortunes and obtained fame that will live on for many, many years after their deaths. I just wonder how powerful their lives would have been had they pursued their callings rather than exploiting their gifts.

As we dig deeper and deeper into our Jesus treasure chest we will see that all the jewels inside only have true meaning if we are using them in alignment with the calling of God upon our lives.

Day 41
Gifts and Calling

I need to back up a step and warn you that just because you have an ability in an area doesn't mean that you should assume that any opportunity that involves that gifting is your specific calling. A few years ago, I was offered a position with an international mission ministry – a position that was very tempting to me because of the opportunity to work closely with some of the cutting-edge advances that are happening in the present-day arena of world evangelism. However wonderful the opportunity might have been, it would have required my full time and total commitment. That meant that I would have to surrender much of the mission work I was doing and the classes I was teaching at the Bible college. As I began to pray about the decision at hand, the Lord directed me to the reference to "gifts and calling" in Romans 11:29. Until that particular day, I had always assumed that gifts and calling were essentially the same; however, I suddenly realized that they are actually two different entities. Our gifts are our God-given abilities; whereas our calling is our divine appointment in life. The gifts are given to us as a means to an end – that end is our calling. In the particular situation I was facing, I was being asked to accept a position that would focus on the gift of administration and organization that God has given me. I could have done the job that was offered to me, and I could have done it very well because I have the necessary gift for the position. However, I would have been neglecting the call upon my life – that of a teacher. Since the whole purpose for the gifting of God in our lives is to serve the calling upon our lives, I knew that I had to turn down the position in order to fulfill a higher purpose.

Day 42

What Makes You Happy?

The next thing that you should ask yourself is what makes you happy. Now, just in case you are tempted to answer, "Sitting in front of the TV with a beer watching football," I'll warn you in advance that this is not the right answer. Perhaps I should phrase the question with the term "joy" rather than "happiness." Joy is the spiritual quality that most closely parallels our human emotion of happiness. It is the reality that we experience in the presence of God Himself. (Psalm 16:11) Of course, God is in your living room when you are watching football, but you are likely not aware of His presence at the moment. However, there are many other times when we experience happiness that seems to penetrate our full being – all the way into our spiritual man. That is the joy that helps us determine where our destiny lies. When you experience such happiness in a task that you would be willing to pay to do it rather than being paid, you've found a career that brings you joy – follow it! That's what Paul did – he found so much fulfillment in preaching the gospel that he ran a side business of sewing tents so he could pursue his passion. He famously wrote to the Corinthians that he would willingly spend and be spent for the privilege of ministering to them. (II Corinthians 12:15)

There are times when we see a need with the excitement of an entrepreneur, relishing the adventure of being the one who has an answer to other people's problems. When this happens, we are filled with a God-ordained joy that jumps out at us telling us that it's time to start rolling up our sleeves because we've just found God's will for our life and are headed toward our destiny!

Day 43

Your Complaints

One other consideration that you should make would be the needs that you see around you. Be aware that we can see needs in a number of different ways and that even negatives can be the gateway to positives.

Someone once said that what you complain about is your divine assignment. Remember that we said that Paul was bothered by what he interpreted to be the rise of a heretical movement – and that this was an indication of his calling into the ministry of teaching and preaching divine truth. So, sometimes it is our negative experience to a situation that prompts us to become the solution.

I always love to illustrate this point by giving the example of a church startup in a rented hotel ballroom. Everyone has worked for two or three hours to get everything ready for the service. They've hauled in all the musical equipment, set up the sound system, and arranged all the chairs. Now, they are all ready to enjoy the praise a worship time and the preaching of the Word. But one mother's crying baby is disrupting the whole atmosphere. Everyone is muttering under his or her breath, "Why doesn't that mother do something about that baby? Doesn't she know that it is ruining our whole service?" That is – everyone but one young lady who is questioning, "That poor baby! Why didn't someone think about renting a second room so there could be a place for the babies and little children to be cared for rather than them having to be held captive in this adult service?" That's the person who is called to start the nursery and children's ministry in the new church!

Day 44
God's Will

As we continue our quest into the seemingly bottomless trunk, the next parcel that we retrieve is titled, "God's will" – exactly what we've been hoping to find! Now, that is reassuring because a couple packages ago we were promised confidence when we prayed according to the will of God. The logical conclusion that we can draw from that is that we are not guaranteed that we will have answers to our prayers if we happen to be praying prayers that are not in accordance with His will. Now we have a promise that tells us that His will is also available in Jesus. Although I Thessalonians 5:18 specifically speaks of thankfulness as an element of God's will that is in Christ, we can extrapolate that there is much more – and, in fact, the entirety – of God's will that is in Christ. If we know that we are in God's will, then our lives have purpose and we know that we have a destiny. Both are guarantees that we can find as we go deeper in Jesus. (II Timothy 1:9, Ephesians 1:4)

> Wherefore be ye not unwise, but understanding what the will of the Lord is. (Ephesians 5:17)
>
> Having made known unto us the mystery of his will, according to his good pleasure which he hath purposed in himself. (Ephesians 1:9)

Many Christians spend their entire lives clueless walking around in a "fog" wishing that they knew the will of God for their lives, But the scriptures clearly tell us that we can and should know what His will is. How to recognize the will of the Lord is one of the most important things that any Christian can ever learn. We can come to know the will of the Lord in several ways.

Day 45
The Word and the Spirit

The first and foremost way to know the will of the Lord is from the written Word. The written Word tells us what is the will of the Lord. For example, it is God's will that none shall perish but that all should come to everlasting life. (II Peter 3:9) If you are seated next to a sinner on the bus, what is the will of the Lord? The will of the Lord is that person next to you should not perish but for him to come to the knowledge of everlasting life. Therefore, the will of the Lord for you is that you should help that person move into the will of the Lord for his life. You don't have to ask God if it is His will for you to share the gospel with that person sitting next to you. You already have His will written in the Word, "Go ye into all the world, and preach the gospel to every creature." (Mark 16:15) The Word of God gives us general direction in what the will of the Lord is. The next step is to allow the Holy Spirit to lead you into God's specific will so that you will know how to approach the individual so as to effectively reach him with the gospel message.

This brings us to another way the Lord reveals His will – through His Spirit. There is an inward witness inside each born-again believer to tell him what God wants for his individual life. God will speak to us; so, it is very important for us to get to the place that we can hear the voice of the Lord. So many people come up to me saying, "If God would only show me what to do, I would do it." It is very likely that He is speaking, and they are not recognizing His voice. When we get very close and personal to the Lord, we are able to hear His voice.

Day 46

The Voice of the Shepherd

Jesus said that His sheep would hear His voice and follow Him but would not follow a stranger. (John 10:3-5, 27) Notice that He said "sheep," not "lambs." We must mature in our relationship with the Lord in order to clearly recognize His voice. We must stay in close communion with Him so we will distinctly know His voice and obey it. Young lovers can talk for three or four hours about nothing at all. When their mothers ask what they have been doing and why they are coming in past their curfews, they reply, "Oh, we were just talking." It was not facts or knowledge that they were communicating; rather, their communication was developing a relationship. The young man received something of the young lady's personality, and she received something of his personality through the time they spent together. Talking is very important in establishing a relationship – with God as well as with other people. We need to get to the place that we can hear the voice of God and – regardless of the circumstances under which that voice comes – we know that it is the voice of God so that we are able to follow through with what He is saying. A mature Christian should be able to recognize the will of the Lord and not to be confused about it.

In Genesis chapter twenty-seven, we find the story of Isaac and his two sons, Esau and Jacob. We know that Isaac was old and blind, but the Bible doesn't say anything about his having hearing problems. Isaac denied Esau's voice because it didn't match with the circumstances. He blessed the deceptive son because he didn't follow the voice that he heard. We should learn a valuable lesson from this Old Testament story – obey the voice of God regardless of the circumstances!

Day 47

Three "C"s to the Will of God
Confirmation, Counsel, Circumstances

Another way that we can know the will of God is through supernatural confirmation. God can use supernatural signs and wonders such as prophecy for confirmation of His will; however, He usually does not give us direction that way. Generally, He uses this form of communication as a confirmation of what He has already spoken into our hearts.

We can also know the will of God through the advice and counsel of elders. When there is something that you want to know or have a question about, bring it up before the eldership in your local church. We don't need to go to a leading televangelist for his opinion on it; we need to go to somebody who personally knows us and loves us enough to give us what is really in his heart. Certainly, the evangelist may have a supernatural word that may relate to us, but our pastor or elder – the person who has seen us mature and has spiritual oversight over us – can go before God with a heart of care for us, and he will receive the answer from God.

One final way of knowing God's will is through the circumstances in which we find ourselves. For instance, Paul certainly didn't plan on getting himself bitten by a snake; but when it happened, he realized that God had set up the circumstances so that a revival could occur on the island. (Acts 28:3-10)

Regardless of the method, it is imperative that we learn to know and follow the will of God for our lives and in our day-to-day affairs.

Day 48

God's Will and His Word

For the sake of solidity in our personal lives, we must also re-evaluate the way we think about the Word of God. The Word of God is a manifestation of the will of God; therefore, we must fill ourselves with it, knowing that it is bringing our lives into alignment with the will and into the favor of the Lord. Jesus said, "If ye abide in me, and my words abide in you, ye shall ask what ye will, and it shall be done unto you." (John 15:7) In other words, having the Word of God dwelling inside of us will guarantee that we will have answers to our prayer requests. First John 5:14-15 explains how this truth works by essentially substituting the term "will" for "words."

> And this is the confidence that we have in him, that, if we ask any thing according to his will, he heareth us: And if we know that he hear us, whatsoever we ask, we know that we have the petitions that we desired of him.

Let's parallel two promises we have concerning our prayers: 1) if we ask according to the will of God, we have confidence that we will have our petitions answered and 2) if we have the words of God abiding in us, we will have our prayers answered. By combining these two truths, we can see that the cognate principle is that the will of God is the same as the Word of God. Being full of the Word will produce a mind that thinks in agreement with the will of God and a life that is lived out in accordance to the divine will.

Day 49
A Lesson for the Prayer Group

I was once part of a group that met early each morning to share requests and then lift up the needs in prayer. Each day they would go around the circle and list all the needs, then one member of the group would be asked to intercede. He would then reiterate all the needs as he mentioned them in prayer to the Lord. Finally, my day came to lead the prayer. I agreed only if they would allow me to do things a little differently. With a nod from the members, I explained that I didn't think that we should spend our time praying the problems but should use the occasion to pray the answers. I challenged each person to give me a biblical promise relating to the need rather than stating the need. Rather than talking about someone's uncle with cancer, I insisted that we talk about the provision Christ had made for the uncle's condition. When I taught them to pray the answer, it changed the entire complexion of the prayer group. They moved from making announcements of bad news to proclamations of the Good News.

> And Jesus answering saith unto them, Have faith in God...Whosoever shall say unto this mountain, Be thou removed, and be thou cast into the sea; and shall not doubt in his heart, but shall believe that those things which he saith shall come to pass; he shall have whatsoever he saith. Therefore I say unto you, What things soever ye desire, when ye pray, believe that ye receive them, and ye shall have them. (Mark 11:22-24)

Day 50

The Trinity

Surprise! The next box we come to is marked, "the entire Trinity"! (Colossians 2:9) The Father, Son, and Holy Spirit are totally in unity in purpose, nature, and action. The wonderful thing about going deeper into Jesus is that we are drawn into the vortex of the Trinity's unity.

Remember, the Father invited the entire Trinity into His initial plan for man when He said, "Let us make man." (Genesis 1:26) In like manner, Jesus guaranteed the involvement of the entire Trinity in His final destiny for the human race, the Great Commission to bring the entire earthly family back into relationship with their heavenly family. But the glory of His plan is that He also invited so us into that grand experience. In Matthew's account, Jesus promised, "Lo, I am with you alway, even unto the end of the world." (verse 28:20) Father. (verse 24:49) In the Acts account, He told the disciples that they would be empowered by the Holy Spirit (verse 1:8), a promise that is apparently intended in Mark's account even though the exact term is not used (verse 16:17-18). John's record of the Great Commission lists the involvement of the total Trinity: the Father sent Jesus, Jesus is sending the disciples, and the disciples are to receive the Holy Spirit. When all these passages are considered at one time, we see a remarkable truth emerging – the total Trinity is involved in empowering us to ensure our success as we go forth to undertake the task Jesus left with us!

> For there are three that bear record in heaven, the Father, the Word, and the Holy Ghost: and these three are one. (I John 5:7)

Day 51
Gifts, Administrations, and Operations

To see how all three persons of the Godhead are involved in our lives, let's take a look at I Corinthians chapter twelve. You may notice that the word "gifts" in verse one is in italic. This means that the word is not actually in the original Greek text. It was added by the translator for what he thought would bring clarity. If we were to translate the verse literally, it would read simply, "I would not have you ignorant concerning spiritual things." Paul does discuss the gifts of the Spirit in this chapter; however, that is not the limit of his interest. He also explains administrations and operations, "There are diversities of gifts, but the same Spirit. And there are differences of administrations, but the same Lord. And there are diversities of operations, but it is the same God which worketh all in all. But the manifestation of the Spirit is given to every man to profit withal." (verses 4-7)

Paul begins by mentioning that the Holy Spirit will give us gifts – supernatural abilities to do things that we as humans would never otherwise be capable of doing. Next, he tells us that the Lord Jesus gives us various administrations. From Ephesians 4:11, we can understand that Jesus is in charge of placing individual believers into positions so that they can minister with the supernatural gifts that the Holy Spirit has placed inside of them. Finally, the apostle turns to the role of the Father and says that He gives us a diversity of operations. Here, Paul is telling us that it is the Father who puts godly motivations in our lives enabling us to function in the positions in which Jesus has placed us, using the giftings that the Holy Spirit has placed in our lives.

Day 52
A Supernatural Message

Paul gives us a listing of the gifts in verses eight through ten, a list of some of the ministry positions (or administrations) in verses twenty-eight through thirty, and a list of the operations in verse thirteen of chapter thirteen: faith, hope, and love. Chapter thirteen emphasizes the futility of the gifts and administrations without the operation of these godly characteristics (verses 1, 2, 3); whereas, verse 12:7 guarantees that there will be universal benefit when all three elements supplied by the total Trinity are in alignment.

Just as I was ready to receive the tithes and offerings in church one Sunday morning, a lady in the congregation stood up and spoke out in tongues. Since I was holding the microphone and was in the position to speak out the interpretation so that everyone could hear, I asked the Lord to give me the meaning of her message. After I had spoken what I felt were the words that the Holy Spirit inspired me to give, we went on with the offering and the rest of the service. It wasn't until the next morning in school that I came to understand the significance of the whole event. When one of my students asked me if I knew what had happened, I replied with, "It was a message in tongues and the interpretation. Of course, we all know how that works." His response to me was astounding, "But, you see, I'm from India, and my native language is Hindi. When the lady spoke, she was speaking in perfect Hindi. When you spoke, you gave the exact word-for-word translation of what she said!" If God wanted so badly to get a message across to the people, He could have simply spoken it audibly over the sound system in the auditorium. But that is not His way of doing things. He always works though human instruments.

Day 53
God Working with Us – and Us with Him

The promise of divine help was actualized in the lives of the first disciples. In addition to the numerous examples we could cite from the accounts recorded in Acts, at least two scriptures specifically say that God actively did His part:

> They went forth, and preached every where, the Lord working with them, and confirming the word with signs following. Amen. (Mark 16:20)
> God also bearing them witness, both with signs and wonders, and with divers miracles, and gifts of the Holy Ghost. (Hebrews 2:4)

The reality of divine involvement is so preeminent that some authors have made the clever play on words, based on the fact that the prefix *co* means "with" that Jesus left us with a <u>co</u>mmission – not just a mission. This is exactly what Jesus was intending when He invited us to be yoked together with Him in His yoke. (Matthew 11:29-30)

In truth, we do better to say that we are on God's team rather than suggesting that He is on our team. Paul clarified the order of significance of team members in I Corinthians 3:9 when he wrote, "For we are labourers together with God: ye are God's husbandry, ye are God's building." In Philippians 2:13, he made it crystal clear that any motivation and any ability to function was not from our side, but totally from God's provision, "For it is God which worketh in you both to will and to do of his good pleasure." In Romans 15:18, he spoke of what Christ had accomplished through him, and it was in Galatians 2:20 that he spelled out the same truth with unequivocal clarity, "I am crucified with Christ: nevertheless I live; yet not I, but Christ liveth in me."

Day 54
He Goes Before Us

In fact, God is much more interested in the Great Commission than any of us as His team members are. He always takes the initiative to "get the ball in play" and then turns to His team members to bring in the score. The story of Cornelius in Acts chapter ten and the story of Saul of Tarsus in Acts chapter nine are great examples of this truth. Notice how Cornelius had a divine encounter and was given a message to go to Simon the tanner's house to look for a man named Simon Peter – even before Peter was made aware that he was a player in this particular game. We have already seen how the same thing happened to Ananias when God pre-committed him to go on what seemed like a suicide mission to find Saul of Tarsus.

> The LORD is the one who goes ahead of you; He will be with you He will not fail you or forsake you. Do not fear or be dismayed. (Deuteronomy 31:8)
> "I will go before you and make the rough places smooth; I will shatter the doors of bronze and cut through their iron bars. (Isaiah 45:2)
> 'The LORD your God who goes before you will Himself fight on your behalf, just as He did for you in Egypt before your eyes. (Deuteronomy 1:30)
> But you will not go out in haste, Nor will you go as fugitives; For the LORD will go before you, And the God of Israel will be your rear guard. (Isaiah 52:12)

Day 55

The Hitchhiker

I often like to illustrate God's strategy by likening it to a football team. The quarterback calls the team into a huddle and directs one player to run down the sideline until he reaches the five-yard line. When the runner makes his turn at the five-yard line, the ball comes to him because the quarterback has coordinated and orchestrated everything to be in perfect syn. All the runner has to do is grab the ball and make a couple steps to score the goal.

The first personal experience of this nature happened when I was a college student back in the 1970s, during the hippie revolution when "sex, drugs, and rock and roll" was the mantra for the day. One day I picked up a young girl who was hitchhiking near the campus. She only needed a lift for a few blocks, but that short ride put her on the most exciting journey of her life – the road to heaven. When she got into my car, she made a comment about the "God loves you" decal on my dashboard. As I began to tell her about the plan of salvation, she shared her story. As an atheist, she had rejected everything anyone had ever shared with her about God or the need for her soul to be saved. However, while experimenting with LSD, she had remained "high" while all the others who were "tripping" with her had come "down." In her drug-induced state, the only explanation she could imagine was that she was dead while all the others were still alive. When she did eventually come "down," she said that something inside of her cried out, "Thank God, I'm alive." At that moment, she knew that she must have a soul and that there must be a God. That divine encounter had prepared her for the conversation I was to share with her that day.

Day 56
The Man in the Painting

When I walked into the Christian bookstore in Delhi, India, the clerk pointed my attention to a picture of Jesus that hung in the front window and said that he wanted to tell me about what had just happened. A Hindu man had come into the store a few days before asking if he could meet the man in the picture. When the shopkeeper explained that it was a painting of a man who lived many years ago, the customer was perplexed, saying that he had seen the man in his dreams several nights in a row and that he knew he needed to meet him. When he saw the painting, he understood that his quest for this mystery man had finally been fruitful. The store clerk, of course, led this hungry soul to salvation.

The most dramatic story of such a divine "hand-off" comes from the remote mountains of Nepal where one of my friends was doing door-to-door evangelism. One man he met in a very isolated mountain village had been having visions of the various Hindu gods. In fact, he had filled numerous volumes with handwritten narratives of all the stories and revelations he had received about these deities. Then one night, he had a vision in which he was directed that he would be given a revelation about a more powerful deity if he would destroy all the journals he had written about the lesser deities. When he burned the other logbooks, he began to have visions and dreams about another god that he had never learned about before. He wrote the stories and revelations about this new god, but didn't have a name for him – until my friend came to his hut and introduced him to Jesus and showed him that the same stories he was recording had already been written down almost two thousand years before!

Day 57
So That's His Name

A little old lady from our church in Indiana traveled into the hinterlands of the Philippines to share the gospel in the unreached villages. In one of these villages, she met a very elderly man who had lived far beyond the normal life expectancy of the people in his area. When Aunty Ruth shared the message of Jesus with the old man, he readily responded with the words, "So that's His name!" He explained that he already knew about this true God through dreams and visions, but had never had an opportunity to know who He was. Only a few days after Aunty introduced him to Jesus, the old man passed away.

Andrew Wommack, the president of the Bible college where I teach, tells the story of introducing himself to a receptionist at a business he was visiting. When she asked what business he was in, Andrew responded that he was a minister. Her next question was, "For whom?" When Andrew replied that he was a minister for Jesus Christ, she immediately interrupted, "Well, then you're the man!" Of course, he questioned her, "What man?" She answered by telling her story. As a Buddhist, she had been going through her religious rituals the night before but felt as if what she was doing was in vain. So she simply prayed, "God, I know that You are real, but I'm not sure who You are. Please show Yourself to me." Instantly, a ball of light invaded her room and a voice spoke to her, "Tomorrow, I'll send a man to tell you who I am." God personally took the divine initiative to reach this woman, but He left the job of scoring the point to one of His ministers. God was <u>working with</u> Andrew Wommack just as He did with the early disciples. (Mark 16:20)

Day 58
Dreams and Visions

Today, there are incredible stories like the ones I've just shared, mostly coming from nations behind the Quran Curtain where Muslim men and women are having supernatural dreams and visions that initiate their quest for the One True God. Because I had heard so many stories about these divine visitations, I decided to investigate a little and asked the audience when I was ministering in the country of Niger, which is almost one hundred percent Islamic, if any of them had had such supernatural dreams and visions. To my surprise almost one fourth of the congregation raised their hands!

God truly is taking the initiative. (John 14:6) He is even more adamant about the Great Commission than we are (II Peter 3:9), but He always passes the ball to His human team members to score the point. Knowing that God is the primary player on the team does take some of the pressure off of us because we realize that we don't have to do it on our own. At the same time, we still need to be vigilant to make our move when the ball is served into our court.

It does no good for a Muslim to have a dream about a man dressed in white unless there is someone who is willing to tell him who that man is. What if no one had built a Christian bookstore in Delhi and hung a picture of Jesus in the window? What if my friend had not gone to the little hut in the remote village of Nepal? What if Aunty Ruth had not climbed over the rugged mountains of the Philippines? What if Andrew Wommack had not stopped to greet the receptionist at that business? What if I had not picked up the hitchhiker? What if you don't follow the Lord promptings today?

Day 59

Paul's Prayers

We are far from emptying our treasure chest, but let's turn our attention to how we access the box itself. Maybe you will remember that my cousins and I never had the key to our grandmother's chest, but there is a scriptural key that can help us unlock this great treasure chest so that we can access all the jewels inside. I suggest that we might start our quest for this key in the prayers of the Apostle Paul. The scriptures actually record four prayers that the apostle prayed for the church. In the first chapter of Ephesians, he prayed that the believers would have the spirit of wisdom and revelation in the knowledge of Christ and that the eyes of their understanding would be enlightened so that they would know the hope of His calling, the riches of the glory of His inheritance, and the exceeding greatness of His power. (Ephesians 1:15-19) In the third chapter of Ephesians, he prayed that they would be able to comprehend and know the love of Christ, which surpasses knowledge. (Ephesians 3:14-21) For the Philippians, he prayed that they would abound more and more in knowledge and judgment. (Philippians 1:9-13) His prayer for the Colossian church was that they would be filled with the knowledge of His will in all wisdom and spiritual understanding and that they would increase in the knowledge of God. (Colossians 1:9-13)

Notice that in these prayers Paul felt that the key to a successful Christian life was knowledge – the same key that Jesus Himself proclaimed, "And ye shall know the truth, and the truth shall make you free." (John 8:32) If we believe error, we will never have the wonderful riches that are stored in the treasure chest; however, once we learn the truth, we can unlock them.

Day 60

Vanity – Part I

But before we actually address the concept of the key of knowledge, let's take a few lines to paint the background so we can see the truth in its proper context. In Ephesians 4:17, Paul directed the believers that they not walk in the vanity of their minds as the gentiles do. Of course, it is easy to immediately define vanity as "emptiness" and go on – totally missing what this verse really has to say. To really catch on to what Paul was trying to communicate, we need to review the book of Ecclesiastes where Solomon defined exactly what vanity entails. In verse 1:14, he concluded that all the works or accomplishments that have been done under the sun are vanity. In verse 2:1, he summarized pleasure and entertainment as vanity. In verse 2:11, he concluded that all forms of employment are nothing more than vanity. Intelligence and education find their way to the vanity list in verse 2:15. Verse 2:17 embraced all of life as vanity. Being in a position of management or authority is also vanity according to verse 2:19. Being in a position to leave behind a legacy or inheritance is also vanity according to 2:21. Verse 2:23 adds diligence and a strong work ethic to the list. Living a moral life falls into the vanity category in verse 2:26. Being human as opposed to simply being a product of evolution still leaves us in the vanity category according to verse 3:19. Verse 4:4 tells us that "keeping up with the Jones" is also vanity. Struggling to make it "up the corporate ladder" falls in the vanity category in verse 4:7. Actually making it to that lonely place "at the top" is also vanity according to verse 4:8. Verse 4:16 describes even the "Rocky syndrome" of the underdog making unexpected achievements as vanity.

Day 61
Vanity – Part II

But we are far from finished with Solomon's list of vanities. Verse 5:10 pulls fiscal security into the discussion of vanity. Verse 6:2 amplifies this truth by adding that – even when it is obvious that wealth is a blessing from God – it can be fleeting and, therefore, vanity. Even long life and a prominent family do not ensure that one's life doesn't end as vanity according to verse 6:4. Verse 6:9 adds desire to the vanity list. Verse 7:6 adds a fool's comments. The inequities between good men and evil men fall on the vanity list in verse 7:15. Verse 8:10 tells us that the things that are forgotten as soon as our obituaries are written are nothing but vanity. The fact that just men seem to get the rewards of the unjust and vice versa is obviously vanity according to verse 8:14. Verse 9:9 says that even a happy home can belie the underlying vanity of the relationship. Verse 11:8 adds that even a long life can be only a camouflage for vanity under the surface. Youthfulness makes the list in verse 11:10. And the concluding summation is that everything is vanity is found in verse 12:8.

That leaves us with essentially "no stone unturned." Business, industry, finance, education, politics, religion, entertainment, family – every area of human interest and endeavor is included as being vanity. Thus, it becomes obvious that the Apostle Paul wasn't saying that the gentiles don't have anything in their brains; rather, he was trying to tell us that the things that they occupy their minds with have no substance. Even if their plans and schemes move nations, transfer fortunes, and change the course of history, they are still vanity in God's sight.

Day 62

The Knowledge of God

In that nothing is left off of the vanity list, we must question what it is that must be planted so that our minds as believers will not be focused on such vanity? Paul answered this question by sharing his own testimony, "Though I might also have confidence in the flesh. If any other man thinketh that he hath whereof he might trust in the flesh, I more: Circumcised the eighth day, of the stock of Israel, of the tribe of Benjamin, an Hebrew of the Hebrews; as touching the law, a Pharisee; Concerning zeal, persecuting the church; touching the righteousness which is in the law, blameless. But what things were gain to me, those I counted loss for Christ. Yea doubtless, and I count all things but loss for the excellency of the knowledge of Christ Jesus my Lord: for whom I have suffered the loss of all things, and do count them but dung, that I may win Christ." (Philippians 3:3-8)

In this passage, Paul gives us a pretty impressive list of accomplishments and pedigrees that would certainly qualify as the "stuff" of success in almost every dimension of life. Yet, he says that all these things are essentially dung – vanity, if you prefer a little more polite description – to him. The one thing that he says is worthy of his consideration is "the excellency of the knowledge of Christ Jesus my Lord." The truth is that the New Testament abounds with confirmations of the fact that the knowledge of God is the essence of the Christian life. (Romans 1:28, 10:2, 11:33; I Corinthians 15:34; II Corinthians 2:14, 4:6, 10:5; Ephesians 1:17, 3:4, 3:8, 3:19, 4:13; Colossians 1:10, 3:10; II Peter 1:2, 1:3, 1:8, 2:20, 3:18)

Day 63
The Christ Hymn

It is the knowledge of our Lord and Savior Jesus Christ that must be planted in us to take the place of the vanity that will otherwise fill the thoughts of our minds and hearts. (Ephesians 3:17 Colossians 1:23, 2:7) But does this mean that we must always go about thinking about God and Jesus like monks cloistered away from the rest of the world in a monastery somewhere? No – a thousand times no! We must find a place of balance where we can continue to live in and have an influence upon all the dimensions of society – yet not be sucked into the vacuum of their emptiness. (John 17:15) The key is to realize that Christ is the true essence of every aspect of life – business, industry, finance, education, politics, religion, entertainment, family, and every other element of life. (I Corinthians 8:6, Ephesians 1:10, Colossians 3:11) The exquisite "Christ hymn" of Colossians 1:14-20 expresses this truth with such grandeur: "In whom we have redemption through his blood, even the forgiveness of sins: Who is the image of the invisible God, the firstborn of every creature: For by him were all things created, that are in heaven, and that are in earth, visible and invisible, whether they be thrones, or dominions, or principalities, or powers: all things were created by him, and for him: And he is before all things, and by him all things consist. And he is the head of the body, the church: who is the beginning, the firstborn from the dead; that in all things he might have the preeminence. For it pleased the Father that in him should all fulness dwell; And, having made peace through the blood of his cross, by him to reconcile all things unto himself; by him, I say, whether they be things in earth, or things in heaven."

Day 64
Really Knowing

But knowing Christ involves much more than mental assent to the truths that we know about Him. Knowing goes far beyond simply hoping or wishing that God is on our side; it involves an unquestionable assurance that comes from actually experiencing the reality of His life in us and our life in Him. Notice in each of the following scriptures from three different New Testament authors writers that each writer tells us that his key is that he <u>knows</u> something:

> My brethren, count it all joy when ye fall into divers temptations; <u>Knowing</u> this, that the trying of your faith worketh patience. But let patience have her perfect work, that ye may be perfect and entire, wanting nothing. (James 1:2-4)
>
> For ye had compassion of me in my bonds, and took joyfully the spoiling of your goods, <u>knowing</u> in yourselves that ye have in heaven a better and an enduring substance. (Hebrews 10:34)
>
> And not only so, but we glory in tribulations also: <u>knowing</u> that tribulation worketh patience; And patience, experience; and experience, hope: And hope maketh not ashamed; because the love of God is shed abroad in our hearts by the Holy Ghost which is given unto us. (Romans 5:3-5)

Day 65
Thoughts That Exalt Themselves Against the Knowledge of God

Let's look at another passage that demonstrates the all-important role of our knowledge of Christ, "For though we walk in the flesh, we do not war after the flesh: (For the weapons of our warfare are not carnal, but mighty through God to the pulling down of strong holds;) Casting down imaginations, and every high thing that exalteth itself against the knowledge of God, and bringing into captivity every thought to the obedience of Christ." (II Corinthians 10:3-5)

For many years, I interpreted this passage to mean that God had given us spiritual weapons to pull down the strongholds established in our lives by thoughts that exalted themselves against the knowledge that God existed – ideas like atheism that says there is no God or Hinduism that says that Vishnu, Krishna, Ganesh, or any one of the other millions of their deities is God, or Buddhism that claims Gautama to be divine, or even New Age that tells us that we all are gods. However, the "Ford Better Idea Light Bulb" came on one day when I realized that the serpent in the Garden of Eden did not challenge God's existence; he simply coerced Eve to accept an inferior view of Him. Before the conversation with the devil in snakeskin, Eve knew God as totally benevolent; after allowing the insinuations of the enemy to infiltrate her thinking, she began to suspect that God had a hidden agenda. She allowed a thought that exalted itself against the true knowledge of God to take a toehold in her mind. Before the conversation was over, it had established a stronghold in her heart, and she was ready to betray Him.

Day 66
Magnifying God

The same is true with each of us, if we allow thoughts that are contrary to the biblical revelation that God is our healer, our provider, our righteousness, our victory banner, and our all-in-all to take root in our minds, we will soon believe that distortion and lose our faith and our relationship with Him. Psalm 78:41 says that the people of Israel limited the Holy One of Israel by not remembering how He had delivered them from Egypt. They allowed thoughts that minimized their God to dominate their minds. If we want to think about God properly, we must always be careful to magnify (Psalm 69:30) rather than to minimize Him and His love for His children. Allow me to define "magnify." When we put a specimen under a microscope or examine it with a magnifying glass, we don't actually change its size; all we do is alter our ability to see it. Magnifying has nothing to do with the reality; it only has to do with correcting our inability to see what already exists. Therefore, when we magnify the Lord, all we are doing is adjusting our view of God.

The Holy Spirit helped me adjust my focus one day when He prompted me to realize that I still harbored thoughts that exalted themselves against God. He questioned me as to what I knew about God. I responded by reciting the redemptive names of God. The Holy Spirit then replied that any time I thought that my healing was in the medicine cabinet I was actually entertaining a thought that was exalting itself against what I knew about Jehovah Rapha and that every time I thought that my provision was in asking my boss for a raise I was again entertaining thoughts that exalted themselves against the true knowledge of Jehovah Jireh – and so on.

Day 67
God's Redemptive Names

Our weapons are strong enough to destroy the arguments against the knowledge of God. There are many areas of truth that we should know about God; however, we often don't comprehend and live in them. We know that God exists, but we fail to attain the true knowledge of who God is and what He does.

God is Jehovah Tsidkenu – the God of our righteousness. The day that Jesus came into our lives, His righteousness came into us. However, the devil will come to each and every one of us with accusations to combat any awareness we have of this righteousness. Just like David's stone found that tiny eyehole in Goliath' armor, the devil will aim for this vulnerable spot. If that lie penetrates into our minds, he begins to build a stronghold against the knowledge of God's righteousness within us.

God is also Jehovah Rapha – the God who heals all of our diseases. The devil wants to plant lies inside us saying that our ailment is either too big for God to heal or too insignificant for Him to notice. The truth is that God is just as willing to heal the little aches and pains as He is to heal major diseases. He is just as able to heal the most dreaded plague as He is to cure a minor ailment.

We can go through all the redemptive names and qualities of God to learn what we should be thinking about God. Any time we allow thoughts contrary to these truths into our hearts, we have permitted the enemy to use his deceit to begin a stronghold in our minds. "Be not conformed to this world: but be ye transformed by the renewing of your mind, that ye may prove what is that good, and acceptable, and perfect, will of God." (Romans 12:2)

Day 68

Epignosis

The Apostle Peter opened his second epistle with a dramatic contrast – offering us two radically different options: the knowledge of God or lust, "Grace and peace be multiplied unto you through the knowledge of God, and of Jesus our Lord, According as his divine power hath given unto us all things that pertain unto life and godliness, through the knowledge of him that hath called us to glory and virtue: Whereby are given unto us exceeding great and precious promises: that by these ye might be partakers of the divine nature, having escaped the corruption that is in the world through lust." (II Peter 1:2-4)

If we choose to pursue the knowledge of God, we are promised an end result of becoming partakers of the divine nature. In other words, the very DNA of God will be evident in our lives. If we chose to pursue lust, it will end in corruption (putrefied ruination). Interestingly, the apostle adds the special Greek prefix epi to both "knowledge" and "lust" making both words intensive so that they should be read "all-encompassing knowledge" and "all-encompassing lust." Think about how your epidermis, or skin, covers your whole body. In the same way that no part of your body is left without a covering of skin (epidermis), no part of our lives should be left without a covering of the knowledge of God (*epignosis*). Just as we are vulnerable to infection If the epidermis is punctured or cut, our spiritual lives are endangered if we are not blanketed with the knowledge of God. The apostle leaves us with no middle ground – either we whole-heartedly seek God, or we will be overwhelmingly swallowed up with lust, greed, and an ever-spiraling desire for more and more material possessions.

Day 69
How We Think vs. What We Think

An insightful glimpse into this scenario of never-ending escalation of self-centeredness came when a reporter asked a billionaire how much would be enough. With a little twinkle in his eye, the financier responded, "Just a little more." In similar fashion, we as Christians must become possessed with an insatiable desire for the knowledge of God rather than a self-centered desire for the things of this world. In the immediately following verses, Peter admonishes the believers to diligently pursue maturity by adding layer upon layer to our spiritual lives, ending with a warning that to fail to do so would result in becoming barren and unfruitful in the knowledge of Christ. Paul presented the identical options in Galatians 6:7-8 when he said that we will reap everlasting life if we sow to the spirit, but corruption if we sow to the flesh.

This all-encompassing knowledge of God is more about <u>how</u> we think about God, not <u>what</u> we think about Him. The issue is not just a matter of knowing that He is all-powerful, but of understanding that He is using this unlimited power to bring blessing and benefit into our lives. We know that God is omniscient – all knowing. However, we can apply that knowledge about His omniscience in different ways. We can assume that since He is all knowing that He knows about all our failures. In this case, we will live our lives in condemnation and defeat. On the other hand, we can apply our knowledge about God's omniscience with an awareness that He knows the intents of our hearts and understands that they are much more noble than the outward failures He has seen. With this in mind, we live victoriously and free of self-condemnation. The key is in <u>how</u> we think about <u>what</u> we know.

Day 70

Cars, Girls, and Money

Proverbs 23:7 proclaims, "As he thinketh in his heart, so is he." Notice that Solomon uses the word "as" indicating that it is how we think – not what we think – that determines who we will be. If what we think about were the determining factor, all American boys would become convertible sports cars by the time they were sixteen; by the time they were twenty-one they would all have turned into girls; and they would all become a million dollar bills by age thirty. In raising my sons, I was keenly aware that my role as their father was to guide them in <u>how</u> to think. Thinking <u>about</u> cars would never make them actually become automobiles, but the <u>way</u> they thought about cars would determine the kind of drivers they would become. I knew that I needed to focus on helping them think of cars as something other than toys, status symbols, and weapons – otherwise, it would be dangerous to be on the road at the same time with them. Thinking <u>about</u> girls would never make them actually become women, but the <u>way</u> they thought about girls would determine the kind of husbands they would become. I knew that I needed to focus on helping them think of girls as something other than sex objects or ego enhancers – otherwise, they would become abusive husbands with no hope of happy, stable marriages. Thinking <u>about</u> money would never make them actually become dollar bills, but the <u>way</u> they thought about money would determine the kind of spenders and investors they would become. I knew that I needed to focus on helping them think of money as a tool to accomplish their goals and as seed for sowing into the future – otherwise, they would be facing a future characterized by unhealthy greed and debilitating debt.

Day 71
New Perspectives

The way we think about God will radically determine the way we live our lives. When I was working in a campus ministry in the 1970s, I traveled – almost like a circuit-riding preacher – from campus to campus, leading Bible study groups. In one of the groups I visited every couple of weeks, there was a young man who was confined to a wheelchair. When I challenged him to believe God for his healing, he said that he felt that God had put him in the wheelchair to keep him humble. I responded, "Keeping us humble is the work of the Holy Spirit, not a wheelchair." That idea was too radical for him to take, so I admonished him to think and pray about it until my next visit. By the time I returned, he had taken the time to reconsider his view of God and now believed that God was a healer, not one who made His subjects sick. When I prayed for him, strength instantly came into his legs, and he was able to abandon the wheelchair altogether! He had been more crippled in his mind than in his legs!

I ended a class on the gifts of the Holy Spirit by asking the students if they felt that God was calling them to operate in any of the giftings. When one young man responded that he felt that he was to operate in healing, I asked if anyone was sick so that he could begin to minister in his calling. One lady had suffered a back injury a number of years before, but was expecting to be healed at a certain evangelist's meeting. I told her that the same God who works in the evangelist's crusades is just as powerful in our little classroom. When she agreed to have her fellow student lay hands on her, she was instantly healed. Her problem was that she was having faith in God's man rather than in God Himself.

Day 72
Hiding in the Trunk

Several days ago, we made mention of Paul's testimony in Philippians chapter three where he declared that his whole aim in life was to know Christ and that he considered everything else in life pointless in comparison to the excellency of the knowledge of Christ Jesus. But today, I'd like to revisit that same passage and pick up on one other goal that Paul had – to be found in Him. (verse 9)

When I read this statement, I envision what would have probably happened had my cousins and I ever had the chance to get into our grandmother's trunk – we would have literally gotten into it! After all, we have all watched little children unpack their Christmas gifts, scatter the toys all over the living room floor, and then crawl into the boxes to play "fort." This is exactly what Paul was expressing – a desire to not only take possession of the gifts in the Jesus treasure chest and to know the Giver of those gifts, but to literally crawl into Him as his fortress and habitation.

In Colossians 3:3, Paul took this concept even one step further when he made reference to our lives being hidden with Christ in God. Not only are we hiding in Christ, we – along with Christ – are also hidden in God. This means that as we go deeper in Jesus, we actually go even deeper into God the Father as well. Of course, none of this happens without walking in the Spirit. The bottom line is that the entire Trinity is beckoning us into ever deepening and more intimate relationship. "When…the Spirit of truth is come, he will guide you into all truth…he shall receive of mine, and shall shew it unto you. All things that the Father hath are mine…he shall take of mine, and shall shew it unto you." (John 16:13-15)

Day 73
From the Roman Jail Cell

Let's make one more visit to Philippians chapter three and notice one additional statement from Paul's testimony. In verses twelve and thirteen, he says that he has not yet attained or even apprehended his goal of knowing Christ and being found in Him. Not only was the apostle aware that he hadn't achieved his goal in life, he realized that he did not even fully understand what it involved! The question that immediately pops into my mind when I read this statement is, "When did Paul make this observation?" Although there is uncertainty as to the actual timeframe in which this epistle was penned, most biblical scholars tend to believe that it was probably written during Paul's Roman imprisonment. In other words, it was during the last few years – or possibly, months – of his life. Paul had lived his full life and completed his total ministry and was still digging deeper into his treasure chest.

The same is true for us. No matter how much we know and experience, there are still more unfathomable depths awaiting us as we go deeper into Jesus. Remember the story about Dr. Lester Sumrall's prayers? Even after more than sixty years, his daily prayer was, "Lord, I want to know You."

It is said that a thousand-mile journey starts with one step. Even though we've spent two and a half months journeying together, we're hardly beyond the first few steps in this lifelong quest to go deeper in Jesus. Keep digging deeper into the Jesus treasure chest!

Teach All Nations Mission

Teach All Nations Mission (TAN) is a global evangelical educational ministry birthed from the teaching ministries of Delron and Peggy Shirley. The name for Teach All Nations Mission was chosen to carefully indicate the exact heart of the Shirleys' mission. TAN's commitment is to establish a solid foundation in national pastors and leaders so they can help enrich their people. This vision is being accomplished by holding national leadership conferences and publishing and distributing Christian teaching materials in English and their local languages.

Someone accurately observed concerning the revival that is occurring in many parts of our world today that it is a mile wide but only an inch deep – the result of energetic evangelism by both missionaries and local Christians. Sadly, there is a marked shortage of teachers who are taking the next step in fulfilling our Lord's directive to teach them how to observe all that He has commanded. Therefore, Teach All Nations Mission has literally taken the words of Christ from Matthew 28:19, "Teach all nations," as its motto and mission statement.

TAN's commitment is to deepen that revival by training the pastors and leaders who then go back and strengthen their congregations. TAN pays for the travel and lodging of handpicked leaders because Delron and Peggy want to invest into their lives but know that these third-world saints could never afford to come at their own expense. TAN always provides the meals for all the guests during these conferences. The ministry also furnishes solid Christian literature in their local language or in English for those who understand the language.

Delron and Peggy realize that the challenge is much bigger than what they can accomplish in person; therefore, they have determined to expand the scope of their vision. One area of expansion includes a scholarship fund that will allow selected individuals to obtain formal education in solid Christian colleges and Bible schools or through correspondence courses. The ministry has also assisted in building a Christian school in Zimbabwe and a Bible college in Nepal. Additionally, Teach All Nations assists the pastors and leaders they work with in times of need such as the tsunami in Sri Lanka, the hurricane in Belize, and the earthquake in Nepal.

Your gifts to and prayers for Teach All Nations will help the Shirleys continue their outreach to Christian leadership around the world.

Teach All Nations Mission
3210 Cathedral Spires
Colorado Springs, CO 8904
719-685-9999
www.teachallnationsmission.com
teachallnations@msn.com

Books by Delron & Peggy Shirley
available at www.teachallnationsmission.com

Bingo – A Fresh Look at Grace
An old joke tells of a man who stood at the Pearly Gates recounting all his good deeds in an effort to gain entry into Paradise. When Saint Peter tallied up the gentleman's score, he did not have anywhere near enough points to qualify. His knee-jerk reaction to the count was, "I'll never get in except by the grace of God." At that instant, the gates swung open and Saint Peter graciously welcomed the gentleman inside. We all know that it is only through grace that we will ever inherit the kingdom of God, but how much do we understand about this all-important subject? Join Bible teacher Delron Shirley as he explores the biblical principle of grace and investigates some of the misconceptions that are current in the Body of Christ today.

Christmas Thoughts
Christmas. The very mention of the word fills our hearts and heads with thoughts – joyous memories, visions of childhood delights, scenes of family gatherings, smells of fresh pastries, tastes of delicious holiday treats, recollections of special friends, strains of favorite carols, and "warm fuzzies" of evergreens, mistletoe, roaring fires, fancy wrappings, shiny decorations, and happy faces. Yes, Christmas is all about thoughts. And we invite you to snuggle up with a hot chocolate and delve into our thoughts about Christmas – and the Christ child whose coming we are celebrating.

Cornerstones of Faith

In our Christian faith, there are also some important cornerstones which serve as foundations to bear the weight of the life we are to build upon them, as indicators or identifiers of who we are as believers, as ceremonial testimonies to the fact that our lives are being built upon Christ, and an unquestionable and invariable standards against which to test and measure everything else in our lives. Proper attention to these essential cornerstones of our faith ensure that our lives rest upon a firm foundation so that we will not fail or falter. Join Dr. Delron Shirley in an examination of the foundation on which our lives must be built.

Daily Devotional Bible Study (five volumes)

This five-volume set of studies takes you on a four-year journey through the Bible. Each manual consists of a walk through the scripture based on studying one chapter each weekday for the fifty-two weeks in a year. Each daily entry includes one verse to memorize. Next comes a short distillation of the basic principle of the chapter and a brief outline of the chapter. This study is intended to be of a rather devotional approach. The Bible study is followed by a simple prayer intended to bring the truth of the chapter into practical application. A section for the reader's notes follows where you can log your own personal revelations and insights about the chapter. A space for logging your own personal spiritual journal (which could include prayer requests, answered prayers, and testimonies) rounds out the daily devotion. The entries for the weekends are a similar format for a study through Psalms. Just twenty minutes a day, seven days a week, fifty-two weeks a year will produce one brand new man in each individual who seriously applies himself to the program and the program to himself.

Daily Ditties from Delron's Desk (Five issues are available)
Each new day comes with its own challenges and blessings. In Daily Ditties from Delron's Desk, you'll enjoy a little pick-me-up to get your day started. So sit back with a warm cup of coffee or tea and see what is in store for you today.

Lessons from the Life of David
In 2004, Michelangelo's famous sculpture, David, went through an extensive cleaning and restoration process in celebration of its five-hundredth birthday. Half a millennium of grime has been removed to once again reveal the majestic splendor with which the masterpiece sparkled when it was first placed in the Piazza Signoria in Florence, Italy. This famous marble statue has often been noted as a most perfect depiction of the human body. And we often think of its subject – the biblical David – as being perfect as well. However, the wonderful thing about the Bible is that it tells the truth -- even about its greatest heroes. They are presented to us as uncovered as Michelangelo's subject, with the only difference being that the Bible depicts its subjects with all their warts, mid-rib bulges, scars, and other defects. In Lessons from the Life of David, Bible teacher Delron Shirley explores both David's triumphs and failures in order to find valuable lessons for our own lives for today.

The Great Commission – DOABLE
While traversing the teeming streets of Kathmandu, Nepal, missionary teacher Delron Shirley was

overwhelmed with the throngs of people who had not yet heard the gospel of Jesus Christ. Looking out at the myriad of faces, it seemed like an impossible task to reach them all. Yet, he knew that Jesus' directive was that the gospel be taken to every human—not just in this one city, but on the entire planet. If reaching this one city seemed like a gargantuan challenge, reaching the planet was beyond imagination! Join Delron in his quest through the scriptures as he explores why the Bible promises that the Great Commission can actually be accomplished and how it is doable in our generation.

Finally, My Brethren

"Finally, my brethren," these are words that seem all too familiar to us when we think of putting on the armor of God for spiritual warfare. However, we often miss the real impact of Paul's message to the church because we have used this as our starting point. But just as we don't start at the top step when we climb a ladder, we can't begin our preparation for spiritual warfare at the last step – putting on the armor. In fact, the Apostle Paul gave us more than fifty steps of preparation to complete before we are ready to get dressed for battle. Join Delron Shirley as he uncovers these often neglected truths. Discover life-transforming truths about your enemy, yourself, God, who you are in Christ, who Christ is in you, and your position in the struggle between the powers of heaven and hell.

Going Deeper in Jesus

In this seventy-three-day devotional volume, Bible teacher Delron Shirley invites you to go with him on a quest into the Jesus treasure chest to discover the unimaginable gifts that God has made available to us in Christ.

The IN Factors

It was offering time in the Sunday school class, and the teacher directed the children to quote a Bible verse about giving as they dropped in their nickels and dimes. A little Afro-American girl with her hair in meticulously cornrow braids grinned from ear to ear as she dropped in the first coin and quoted, "It is more blessed to give than to receive." Her redheaded, freckle-faced friend shyly blushed as she added to the coffer while mumbling, "Give and it shall be given back to you." Next, a young guy tossed in what might have been his "tooth fairy money" as he flashed a broad smile that exposed the spot where his front tooth had been last Sunday. He then recited, "The Lord loves a cheerful giver." As the fourth little fellow stumbled through, "The seed in the good soil brought forth thirty-, sixty-, and one-hundred-fold return," the teacher anxiously eyed the next child – a first-time visitor who had not been schooled in any of the "giving" passages. Anxious over the fact that the guest would be embarrassed, her heart raced a bit as the offering basket reached him. As the reluctant little tyke begrudgingly plunked in his contribution, he blurted out, "A fool and his money are soon parted."

Although the visitor's quote wasn't from the Bible, it was apparently more appropriate in his own case than any of the verses with which the teacher had coached the rest of the pupils. The truth is that most of us, like the students in the elementary class, have been taught only part of the lesson of what God wants us to know about finances. In The IN Factors, Bible teacher Delron Shirley invites you to join him as he explores some of the lessons that have been taught – but equally important – truths on the topic.

In This Sign Conquer
Marching toward an enemy that he wasn't sure he could defeat, Constantine questioned himself, his army, his military abilities, and even his deities. Then suddenly something happened that changed his life. No, something happened that changed the whole history of Western civilization. He saw a vision in the sky of the Christian cross accompanied by the words, "In this sign conquer." Abandoning his pagan gods and accepting the cross of Christ as his battle insignia, he marched into the Battle of Malvian, defeated Maxentius, and took the throne of the Roman Empire. Since none of us was there in AD 312, we can't be certain how sincere the new emperor was in his acceptance of the cross as his victory symbol. However, we must know that there are signs and symbols that God has given to each of us to ensure our victory and success in life. Join Bible teacher Delron Shirley as he explores this fascinating topic.

Interface
This book should be viewed as an anthology because each of the seven studies was written at a different time with no deliberate connection to the other six. However, there is a thread running through these independent studies that ties them all together as they communicate different aspects of one unified message – being strategic in our spirituality. The first study deals directly with the interfaces discussed in the Bible where we connect with the world around us, the kingdom of heaven, and the kingdom of darkness. The second study in the series discusses finding the sensitive balance between two necessary interfaces – our need to spend time with God and our mandate to rise up and interact with the world. The third and fourth

studies have to do with the biblical truths that we need to understand in order to accurately interface with our God, our world, and ourselves. In the letters to the seven churches of Asia Minor recorded in Revelation chapters two and there, only one of the churches is specifically mentioned as being at an interface; the church at Philadelphia is said to have an open door set before it. Interestingly, this is also the only church that is specifically mentioned as having a relationship with the Word of God. (Revelation 3:8, 10) Therefore, it is significant that we take some time to explore some foundational biblical truths that we must stand upon as we approach the various interfaces set before us. The fifth study takes us through the life of one of our most beloved biblical heroes—David, the shepherd boy who killed a giant and wrote beautiful psalms. Although his life was riddled with one failure after another, he somehow attained the report that he was a man after God's own heart, which is the key to opening the doors of interface with the world that we learn about in the letter to the Philadelphian church. (Revelation 3:7) Next, we look at what it really means to have heart after the very heart of God – one that Bob Pierce, founder of World Vision, described as being broken with the same things that break the heart of God. Finally, the book concludes with a challenge to never fall short of the opportunities and blessing that God has provided for us as we interface with the One who sent us and those with whom we are to interface.

Israel – Key to Human Destiny
The Jewish people and the nation of Israel are puzzles and enigmas in world politics and human logic. How can it be that a group of people who account for less than one half of a percent of the world's population is

responsible for one out of every five Nobel Peace prizes? Israel is so tiny a territory that no world map can even squeeze its name on the space allotted it on the layout, yet this minuscule nation dominates our evening news every night. Why is it that one little country of only a few million people can tie up the wealth, the foreign policy, and the political movements of the greatest nations on the face of the earth? Why is it that of all the ethnic groups in the world, only one bears the stigma (or honor) of having its name specifically coined into a word of hate and antagonism: anti-Semitism? The answers to these puzzling questions lie in the fact that these are no ordinary people and this is no ordinary piece of real estate. These are covenant people living in covenant land. Their destiny is charted by prophetic words from God Himself. Indeed, the saga of all mankind revolves around this people. Israel is the key to the human drama. Join Delron Shirley as he journeys into the past and glimpse into the future in order to understand the present.

The Last Enemy
Fear? Death? Defeated!! The Bible declares that death is our ultimate enemy and that the fear of death is a cruel warden that can hold us in the chains of slavery and bondage throughout our lives. BUT, our enemy Death has met his Waterloo and can no longer hold us in his power. In The Last Enemy, explore Passover weekend AD 33 changed your destiny.

Lessons Along the Way
Welcome to a journey that will lead you across the towering Himalayan Mountains, over rushing waterfalls, and into your own backyard. At each step of the

journey and around each bend in the path, you will discover the most exciting thrills of life – not the rush of adrenalin released while crashing through the rapids of the Grand Canyon, not the spine-tingling chill of coming face-to-face with demonic supernatural forces, not the awesome hush of grandeur inspired by the majestic sunsets across the glacier polish of the majestic Sierra Nevada range – although all these and much more are included. You will discover the thrill of hearing the voice of God Himself speaking to you for direction and encouragement. Join us on this fascinating journey through life. Be ready to learn all the lessons along the way!

Living for the End Times
"The end is near!" "Jesus is coming back!" "These are the last days!" We all have heard these prophecies. Sometimes, we've heard them so often and over such a long period of time that they may have lost their impact. Yes, we believe that these are the last days, but we somehow keep living as if we think that things will always keep going as they always have and that nothing is ever going to change. Is it possible that we have given mental ascent to the concept of the end time but never let it really get hold of our lives? Let's explore what it means to live our lives as if we really believed that these are the end days – after all, they really are!

Maturing into the Full Stature of Jesus Christ
As a child, I learned a little song in children's church: "To be like Jesus, to be like Jesus. That's all I ask – just to be like Him." When I grew up, I realized that there was a whole lot more to becoming like Christ than just singing a little children's song. It has been said

that going to church doesn't make you a Christian any more than sitting in the garage will make you an automobile or sitting in a donut shop will make you a policeman. There is a maturing process that we must go through if we ever hope to manifest the true nature of Christ in our lives. That maturing process demands that we have a total transformation in the way we think – that we be brainwashed, if you will. It requires more than just saying the right words; after all a parrot can speak English, but he is not an Englishman. In the same way, we must not settle for just learning the Christian jargon; we must be transformed into the very likeness of Christ through the renewing of our mentalities. You may not be what you think you are, but what you think – YOU ARE! Join Bible teacher Delron Shirley as he investigates how the way we think determines who and what we will be. Learn how your thinking can transform you into the full stature of Jesus Christ.

Maximum Impact
He showed up totally unannounced with no publicity agent, no campaign manager, and no budget to fund a campaign. Yet within three short weeks, he established a viable community of faith that was soon acknowledged and recognized as a role model throughout the world. Who was this man, and how did he flip the world one hundred eighty degrees on its axis? Join Bible teacher Dr. Delron Shirley as he makes a fascinating quest into the man, his methods, and the mission of a man who left maximum impact everywhere he went.

Of Kings and Prophets – Shapers of the Destinies of Nations
Bible teacher Dr. Delron Shirley invites you into his time machine to travel back through the corridors of time to visit the era of the Old Testament kings and prophets in the nations of Israel and Judah – the men who shaped the destinies of their nations. In walking through the encounters, interactions, and conflicts in the lives of these historical figures, we are constantly reminded of the words of the New Testament writer who said that everything that happened in the lives of these men serves as an example and a caution to us so we can make a difference in our own generation.

Passion for the Harvest – A Missions Handbook
We all know the Lord's statement that the harvest is plenteous but the laborers are few. However, I would like to suggest a little different consideration of the situation: the harvest is plenteous but the laborers are untrained. The cover photograph of a Nepali woman harvesting her grain not only pictures the primitive conditions in which the third world harvests their physical grain, it also helps us get a glimpse of the need for the entire Body of Christ to be trained for the spiritual harvest as well. In Passion for the Harvest, Bible teacher Delron Shirley exposes some of the pertinent truths necessary for preparing us for the challenge of the harvest. Learn how to sow in order to reap an abundant harvest and how to discern the harvest that the Lord is sending your way. Learn how to develop the resourcefulness and the expectant hope necessary to stand steadfastly until the harvest manifests and we discover new truths concerning the tools and the stamina necessary for reaping the full harvest. In short, develop a passion for the harvest!

People Who Make a Difference

Have you ever noticed that there are some people who just seem to stand out from the crowd? Although they may seem ordinary in so many ways, there is just some special something about them that identifies them as unique individuals. Though they may not be the "movers and shakers" that we think of as the ones who can push their way to the top of the corporate ladder, they somehow wind up leaving an indelible mark on their worlds. Let's explore what it is that makes some people the ones who make a difference. Better yet, let's learn how to be those individuals!

Positioned for Blessing and Power

In the first Psalm, David gave us a formula for a life that qualifies for God's blessings – be careful about where you walk, sit, and stand. In the book of Ephesians, the Apostle Paul gave us a formula on how to live in the power and authority of God – be determinate about where we sit, walk, and stand. In <u>Positioned for Blessing and Power</u>, Bible teacher Delron Shirley combines these two principles – one from the Old Testament and one form the New – in a way that can revolutionize your life.

Problem People of the Bible

In <u>Problem People of the Bible</u>, you will meet many of the biblical characters you have had to skip over as you did your daily reading because you simply couldn't understand exactly how their lives figure into the message of God's love and plan of salvation. This insightful story will help you make sense of their place in the grand scheme of the Bible and the story of God's dealings with the human family.

So, You Wanna Be A Preacher
A distillation of Delron Shirley's twenty-five years of mentoring young ministers and the evaluation of over ten thousand church services and sermons, So You Wanna Be A Preacher covers a wide range of topics from how to recognize and respond to the call into the ministry to tips on preparing and presenting your sermons and on getting them published. Special emphasis is given to helping you understand the minister's job description and recognizing how to manifest the Holy Spirit's presence in your ministry. The minister's personal life including discussion of ethics and etiquette is a major focus in the study. No matter what your ministry or calling, you are guaranteed to get new insights in your role as a minister and gain some helpful hints into effectively serving the Lord and His people.

Tread Marks
Does your life leave a mark on the people you meet and the circumstances you find yourself in? In Tread Marks, you'll learn a number of where-the-rubber-meets-the-road principles of successful Christian living that are guaranteed to ensure that you will leave a positive impression on individuals and society. Based on biblical principles and true life experiences, this book grapples with everyday life issues and presents simple but effective approaches to facing them successfully and victoriously. From the stories of the sinking of the Titanic and an African safari adventures to the expositions on Joshua's conquest of the Promised Land and Joseph's rise from slavery to the second most powerful man in Egypt, you'll be entertained, inspired, and motivated. You'll discover how your life can make a lasting impression.

A Verse for the Day (Two Issues are available)
In A Verse for the Day, Bible teacher Delron Shirley brings you a new insight into the Word of God each day with observations about the unique contributions the selected verses can make in our lives. Though the studies of these verses are by no means comprehensive or exhaustive, the fresh insights you'll gain in these daily visits with the Word of God are guaranteed to encourage, challenge, and inspire you in your walk with the Lord.

Women for the Harvest
"God's secret weapon" – that's how many people are coming to realize that we, as women are in the world of ministry. One example is, Dr. Yonggi Cho, who has the second largest church in the world. He has been quoted as saying, "Women are the greatest evangelistic tools. Someday the church will catch on." In this volume, author Peggy Shirley does an in-depth study into the history of why women have been forbidden from taking their God-given place in the church and explores the powerful biblical and historical examples of what happens when women are allowed to use the giftings which God has placed inside them. A revealing study of the scriptures which have long been used to block women from service, coupled with a motivational study on how to break free from the bondages which have held women back and a wealth of practical suggestions and advice -- this book is guaranteed to release you to become a true laborer in God's end-time harvest.

You'll be Darned to Heck if You Don't Believe in Gosh *and Other Musings*
This eclectic collection of mediations and musings addresses many issues concerning our Christian faith, including exactly what the Bible teaches about hell and who will go there, how prayer works, and how we should understand exactly who Jesus is. This study also takes you on a spiritual journey that delves into such topics as simple advice for Christian leaders and the biblical formula for radical change – both in your own personality and in the complexion of a whole nation.

Lighthearted at times, but always simple and straight forward, this refreshing study makes discovering theological truths from the scripture fun and enlightening. Buckle your seatbelt as you join Bible teacher Delron Shirley as he journeys to such interesting places as Nepal and Nigeria in quest of spiritual insight and revelation. You'll be glad that you came along for the adventure as you discover many simple truths that have always seemed just too difficult to understand.

Your Home Can Survive in the 21st Century
Have you ever heard someone say that we should get rid of old fashion ideas about marriage, family, and morals and add "After all, it is the twenty-first century"? With the rapid decline in traditional values, we might actually begin to question if our home will be able to survive in this new century. But there is good news if we only recognize that what is happening to the family today is a prophetic attack by the forces of the devil and that we are well equipped to fight back and conquer! Your home can not only survive – it can thrive!!

www.ingramcontent.com/pod-product-compliance
Lightning Source LLC
LaVergne TN
LVHW051150080426
835508LV00021B/2569